GUARANTEED RETIREMENT

GUARANTEED RETIREMENT

SECRETS OF THE RICH AND FAMOUS
FOR PRESERVING YOUR WEALTH

John STEVENSON

THE GUARANTEED RETIREMENT GUY

GUARANTEED RETIREMENT
Secrets of the Rich and Famous for Preserving Your Wealth

ISBN: 978-1-956220-41-4

Expert
Press
www.ExpertPress.net

Editing by Tamma Ford
Copyediting by Lori Price
Proofreading by Abby Kendall
Text design and composition by Emily Fritz
Cover design by Casey Fritz

Dedicated to my beautiful wife, Holly.
When it comes to guarantees, nothing compares to
her constant unwavering support and love.

Contents

Who Am I and Why Listen to Me?

I AM A MAN OF FAITH, FAMILY, AND FINANCE.

A defining experience for me in my faith was my mission. As a young man, I decided to serve a mission for my church, the Church of Jesus Christ of Latter-day Saints. It was a two-year commitment, and I paid for it myself; that was about $9,000 back then. I worked seventy to eighty hours a week knocking on doors, talking with people, serving people, doing community service. Serving and learning to be selfless was a big takeaway for me.

Learning how to focus more on others than myself was priceless. It was a great experience in my life and in my faith.

I had a lot of thoughtful guidance from older people when I was growing up, and this was the first time I could give back or pay it forward (however you wish to look at it). As a young boy and teen, I was in Boy Scouts; as an adult, I've coached young men in Scouting and in my church. I try to continue to pay it forward while working with and mentoring youth. It is very rewarding to see young people (including my own children) thrive in the world with confidence. Every individual is unique and valuable. I try to communicate and live that for the young men I coach and for my own children.

I encourage young people to open up to their talents and passions. I love to sing and act. I trained professionally to sing for over twenty years. I was even privileged to learn from the late Michael Jackson's voice teacher for a while. I have done musicals, music competitions, and various solo and special arrangement performances over the years. I really loved being able to perform and to move people, to change lives by the way I performed. I'm also an avid hiker and love the great outdoors. When I'm not working, I'm usually in the mountains, backpacking, skiing, snowboarding, or otherwise adventuring. When I am in nature, my other stresses and concerns fade away.

I'm big on family, although it did take me five years before I finally decided to ask my wife to marry me! But I always knew I wanted my own family and children. We've been married for fourteen years now and are blessed with five beautiful children. My wife's an amazing woman. I consider my marriage and my family life to be great achievements. Our youngest is just six months old as I write this, meaning I'll be sixty when my last child leaves the nest (barring any future births!).

In the realm of finance, I got my start as an entrepreneur building a window-cleaning business from scratch in Las Vegas. I was twenty-three. I went around and knocked on doors, talked to people, and didn't always know what I was doing—except that I knew how to wash a window! During the time I built that company, it was able to grow by double digits ten years straight and produce millions in revenue.

By year six, I was working around five to ten hours a week in the business; the systems and staff enabled that to happen. Nonetheless, I did get burned-out over time. Dealing with employees and all the challenges that came with them got old.

After a decade, I sold the business for $733,000, which felt awesome to be able to build something from nothing to later sell it for so much. Had I known what I am about to teach in this book, I would have invested that money quite differently. You see, when it comes to the piles of cash we have . . . whether it be from selling a business, an inheritance, a 401(k) or similar savings plan, we need a plan to *keep* the money and also be able to leverage it for *guaranteed* income—income that lasts as long as we do.

A couple of years later, I started again in Reno, Nevada. I built the same business but five times faster, using the systems that had already worked for me. I was able to build its annual revenue up to $250,000 in just one year. At the end of that year, I sold the business for almost $200,000 cash. Again, it felt great to see my proven systems work in another market!

The reason I share this is because after I sold those companies, I essentially *lost* all of that money due to bad ventures/investments. I have often asked myself what I would have done different with that money if I could just go back in time!

Also, during this time, I moved into coaching thousands of people all around the US and the world on how to build not just a profitable window-cleaning business, but any service business and make it profitable. I found that I liked helping others succeed faster than I did by helping them remove the learning curve. Similarly, I have been able to coach many retirees on how to maximize their guaranteed retirement income while removing the risks that I myself had fallen into earlier. This is why I do what I do, and it is extremely fulfilling!

As a coach and an educator, I teach classes on Social Security, estate planning, and retirement tax planning in universities and colleges throughout Nevada. I am also the host of *Retirement & Income Radio*, which airs each week to my listeners in southern Nevada. In that show, I'm able to teach safe money and guaranteed retirement principles to help retirees and investors think about money and income.

Someone once told me that as an advisor, I am one of the three most important individuals people talk to when their loved one dies. They go to their family.

They go to their pastor or their church. And they go to their financial or retirement planner—me. As a Certified Financial Fiduciary, I take the responsibility very seriously. My goal is to affect people positively and be able to help them create a retirement that guarantees the income they need for the rest of their lives—no matter how long they live. I started providing tax-free wealth and retirement consulting services to clients in 2002 and have learned a lot along the way.

I am motivated to help people have the best financial retirement they can. I'm also motivated to give them the most choices and accurate information I can so they can make the best choices for their circumstances. I'm not here to sell every client the same product day in and day out. I can show them all the products in the market, and I do. I help them analyze the advantages and disadvantages of various financial solutions so they can make their own informed decisions. It's very gratifying for me to be able to help many people feel and be financially secure in their retirement years.

I'm licensed in insurance and have become an expert in structuring tax-free retirement accounts and fixed index annuities, which help my clients build wealth safely while enjoying an extremely low tax burden (or even zero taxes) in retirement. If you'd like some help, please send me a message at john@johnstevenson.com.

As a man of faith, family, and finance, I have written this book to show you why so many people are building wealth safely, enjoying income guarantees at retirement, and enjoying their retirement without stress and worry. You too can enjoy this type of wealth and create guaranteed income for life—income that you can never outlive.

1

Guarantees and Risk

"THERE ARE NO GUARANTEES IN LIFE." I'm sure you've heard that warning. We usually hear it from some well-intentioned person near and dear to us when one of our plans hasn't worked out the way we hoped it would!

I disagree somewhat with that warning because, as you've noticed from the title of my book, guarantees are part of my topic. I'd like to look at why there are so few guarantees, particularly, in your financial life, and it's summed up in one word: *risk*.

I realize that you have probably thought a lot about risk, but let's review one more time the three kinds of risk to pay particular attention to as you approach retirement. Three? Yes, most people I talk to invest their money for growth or retirement income in one of three common ways. Let's look at financial market, business, and real estate risk.

Financial Market Risk

Market risk is when your assets are directly invested in the financial market, such as the US or other global stock markets. You usually have an investment portfolio that has your money directly invested into stocks, bonds, mutual funds, exchange-traded funds (ETFs), or perhaps a variable annuity.

Market risk recognizes that your assets are subject to all the market's fluctuations, both up and down. The only "guaranteed floor" is zero (unless you are investing on margin, then it could go negative quickly on a bad day). When you invest any money in the financial markets, there is a chance you could lose your entire investment. In other words, I'd call that risky!

Most people who invest for their retirement do so through employer-sponsored retirement plans, such as a 401(k), 457(b), 403(b), Thrift Savings Plan (TSP), and others. In these accounts, you are limited to whatever investment funds the employer-sponsored plan has. If you're young enough, you have plenty of time to ride out market downturns and are also able to take advantage of rises in the market; while you are younger, you usually don't care that much when the stock market drops hard. The up-and-down volatility can be your friend when you are a young saver and help you build tremendous profits. You have time to seize this advantageous volatility when you are a couple of decades away from your retirement. When you are five to ten years from your retirement, you usually don't have time to recoup losses. Most advisors agree that reducing risk to your portfolio five to seven years from retirement is the best.

Real Property and Real Estate Risk

It's not just financial market risk you need to look at. You're subject to *real estate market* risk if you own a house or any investment property—even when you count on selling your primary residence to fund your retirement.

This market can be as volatile as the financial markets. When the housing market drops (and it does, in a cyclical but not always predictable manner), rents tend to go down. If you are a landlord, then your return on investment is lower than anticipated and may even be less than your costs (mortgage, insurance, etc.).

As far as managing real estate market risk and housing appreciation goes, if you are determined to stay in, then stay in for the long haul. The best way to manage real estate market risk is (probably) not to leverage yourself but certainly not overleverage yourself. We all remember during the 2008 housing crisis when many investors lost everything from being overleveraged. Calculate all your holding costs, including those of hiring a property management company. As in the financial markets, ride out the lows, and you'll still be there for the rises.

Again, when nearing your retirement, you can't bank on having enough time to ride out declines! We do not know what the future holds. So, in the here and now, you protect what you have.

Business Risk

If any entrepreneur ever doubted it, the COVID-19 pandemic showed us there is a risk to *owning a business*.

Having owned multiple businesses, I've been able to experience market and economy declines that can affect a business greatly. As a business owner, you have to be very nimble. Some retirees plan to have their business cover their retirement but don't think about the risks involved in continuing to run it or turning it over to someone else as they get older. They also don't realize, with time and age, that owning and running a business and all the time it takes was not what they had in mind for their golden years!

Many retirees cash out their 401(k)s to purchase a business, only to find they lack the skills to keep the business afloat or grow it. They were willing to take the *risk* for the potential rewards of owning a business into retirement. If you are counting on business income to fund all or part of your retirement, you need ways to mitigate the risks to your business's profitability and relevance.

Protect What You Have

The bottom line is that older investors—anyone five to ten years from retirement—need to manage risk to their money. Older investors need to remember that when any of these investments drop dramatically (and this periodically happens), it usually takes five to seven years for values to rise again to their starting point.

For instance, with the 2008 crash, it took around six years for everyone's account to get back to breakeven. If you'd projected to retire in 2008, your financial market portfolio might have decreased to the point where you put off retirement! Do you want to delay retirement as much as six years? Most people don't.

When you enter retirement, you just want to know that your nest egg is protected and pays your way for the rest of your life. You also want to know you are getting the highest income you possibly can from any investment you make. Any type of risk makes this goal something that's not guaranteed!

The first rule of investing is to conserve your principal, which means keeping your money away from high-risk investments. As you approach retirement, this might mean pulling much of your nest egg out of a fluctuating investment and into more protected ones. In other words, you need to manage your market risk *much differently* as you get older, or you might see your lifetime of hard-earned savings dwindle or even disappear entirely.

If you are willing to change the way you have placed and invested your money just a little bit, you can ensure that your money lasts as long as you live.

If You Still Need a Reason

I've got three reasons for you *not* to keep your *entire* nest egg in a bank or in any of the risky markets I've mentioned.

- REASON #1: The stock market and all its component investments go up or down. You don't know how much the downward fall might be. No one can ever know how long it will take for the markets to rise again.

  You might say, "I have all my money diversified," but don't be fooled. This strategy can fail or suffer downturns as well.

  Likewise, if your money is in preferred stock, the companies paying dividends are in control of those amounts; companies can change them downward at any time or eliminate the dividends altogether.

- REASON #2: Having your money in a bank or trading account, especially the latter, means you need to continuously manage it.

  Many types of investments, from municipal bonds to individual stocks, require your attention. It requires ongoing management for you (and possibly your spouse if you pass away). You (or your spouse) may not have the expertise or time to do it. That means you need to pay someone to manage it, which means you're losing part of your nest egg profitability as you pay them for their management expertise.

The same management burden can apply to real estate holdings. Investment property is rarely a "passive" investment.

- REASON #3: If you're married and you manage all of the finances, and it's sitting in various accounts, does your spouse know what you're doing? Can your spouse continue to manage it in your place if you die or become incapacitated?

  The types of investments and contracts I will be explaining in the following chapters can provide solutions to the above concerns. They typically provide contractual, guaranteed income every year for the rest of your life. There is no downside risk to your nest egg, and no management is required on your part.

Guarantees

I just read on my news feed (in January 2023) that a French nun (Lucile Randon) died a few weeks before her 119th birthday. Wow! Two questions come to mind: How many of us can even *imagine* living that long, and what was her financial picture all those years? Then two questions I would ask you are how long will you live, and how long will you need to fund *your* retirement? You just don't know! You may be the first centenarian or supercentenarian of your family. You can't know for sure, but you should not rule out the possibility.

There's no telling how long you'll live. But whether you've been earning your living from being a baker or businessman, a physician or farmer, a nun or nuclear physicist, you can absolutely guarantee your money lasts as long as you do; I'm going to tell you, in the remainder of these pages, how to do just that.

You can't outlive the guaranteed retirement stream(s) of income I'm going to present next. The income will be coming in predictably and regularly to support your lifestyle *no matter how long* you live.

What is guaranteed income?

Guaranteed retirement income is a stream of money that flows to you all the years of your retirement without fail. *Guaranteed* means one thing: You cannot outlive the income—even if you live until age 119.

There is no way you can run down the balance of a guaranteed stream of income the same way you can with a large sum of cash stashed away in some bank account. Remember: There is no guarantee your bank and trading accounts will not drop to zero dollars in ten to twenty years down the road. *The guarantee is almost always that the money won't last as long as you do!* And then? You have no more cash for the rest of your life. At that point, you have to go back to work or move in with your family. Most people don't want that.

If you're close to or at retirement, you've probably saved a decent amount of money, and if you are like many of my clients, you don't know what to do with that big pile of cash. Most advisors will tell you to take smaller amounts from it over time, and then diversify it for growth and protection. Usually, they don't warn you against any market fluctuations, inflation, or other outside forces that will affect the balance and your annual income needs.

So, instead of funding your retirement needs directly from it, you could turn it into guaranteed income—for life. This is about creating a dependable, recurring, continuous stream of income you'll get for the rest of your life—for however many years you may live.

As alluring as the word *guaranteed* seems, people don't always see the beauty of this retirement funding solution right away.

As a retirement planner, my number one rule is to always help you protect your principal—to reduce risk to your nest egg. My number two rule is to create enough income for life. In the following chapters, I'll show how you can do this and guarantee a retirement income for yourself for life. With safety. With predictability. And with peace of mind.

I'll talk about two main options you should consider, and then I will compare and contrast them with other options you may now be using. They are:

- Fixed index annuities
- Tax-free retirement accounts or TFRAs

I'll also show you how to do some "laddering" with your annuities to:

- maximize your Social Security benefits.
- increase your income *during* retirement and to beat inflation.

2
Annuities

BEAR WITH ME. I know after reading the name of this chapter, you're saying, "John! Please! Annuities? Are you kidding? Who would touch those?"

I get it. People have a good reason for not liking annuities because back when they were first introduced, they were almost all *variable* annuities. These types of annuities were subject to market fluctuation and significant risk. There are still variable annuities out there, but they are not as popular as they once were. Another reason people don't like them is the cost (which can be up to 4 percent annually when you factor in all of the fees).

Annuities are insurance contracts issued by life insurance companies. You purchase them with a lump sum or monthly contribution (more common in 403(b) and similar plans). This money is invested, and at some future time, the insurance company will begin paying regular income payments, either for a fixed period or for the rest of your life (this is sometimes called the "annuitization period" or "lifetime withdrawal benefit").

Annuity Basics

An annuity is a legal document between you and a life insurance company. This agreement or contract can help you generate additional earnings based off an external index and take advantage of tax-deferred gains. Tax deferral benefits you because it can help you accumulate wealth faster for various long-term goals, including retirement.

Life *insurance* is not the same as a life *annuity*.

- Life insurance policies protect individuals and families from financial loss if their primary breadwinner passes away unexpectedly, while life annuities are used to help fund people's retirement needs who are expected to live a long life.

- Life annuities guarantee you a fixed periodic income stream that you can't outlive.
  As a result, if you choose to take income payments for the rest of your expected life, you will have a source of income the entire time that you can count on.

An annuity consists of an accumulation phase and a payout phase. This means that once you purchase an annuity, your insurance company will pay you a specified income for an agreed-upon time frame— often for life. This can be immediate, which is an immediate annuity, or after the accumulation period has been reached, which is a deferred annuity. Once you "annuitize your annuity," that is, begin to receive regular income payments from your annuity, you cannot adjust your payments or withdraw money from the principal unless you turn off the guaranteed lifetime income payment.

Also note that, in contrast to life insurance applications, annuity applications don't require any proof of good health or medical underwriting to be approved. Approval is more related to your overall financial health.

Annuities are guaranteed by life insurance companies. The account value of the annuity is the death benefit, but its main purpose is usually to provide a specified guaranteed income from the policy. The life insurance company is basing its guaranteed payout on current mortality tables, so age and life expectancy are the primary factors in how they work.

The advantages of annuities are huge. Many people don't like them at first glance because they were either taught that all annuities are bad, or they just don't understand them. This, unfortunately, came from a lot of misinformation decades ago, when variable annuities were the most popular. For my clients who are looking for preservation of their capital, access to growth, and an income stream they can't outlive, I prefer a *fixed index annuity with an income rider attached.*

A commission-minded professional might sway you towards a variable annuity by stating, "You can get guaranteed income and all the huge market returns at the same time!" What they don't mention are all the fees that greatly reduce your "huge market returns" of 8–10 percent into 4–6 percent real return on investment (ROI) after you've paid their fees.

What I'm focusing on here is the *fixed index annuity* (FIA) whose average fees are around 1 percent a year, which is the average that many advisors charge already. The difference is, instead of paying a fee to an advisor (regardless of if your account suffers a loss), you're paying a fee that actually benefits you directly because it ensures that you have a guaranteed income payout now or later. The insurance company also invests about two-thirds of your principal balance into high grade bonds to pay for the guarantees in the contract and to earn them a profit. The remaining one-third is used to purchase call options associated with a particular index to give you access to credited gains if that index value goes up. This is why you don't ever lose a dime of your principal when markets tank, while still having access to significant growth potential when the index is rising.

Fixed index annuities are also one of the greatest ways to create guaranteed retirement income—income that lasts as long as you live. Income that comes in regardless of what the market is doing. Income that comes in with no effort or management on your part.

If you are an educator and contributing to a Teachers Insurance and Annuity Association (TIAA) sponsored retirement plan, you may already know that some or all of your account could be an annuity and, upon retirement, can give you either a lump sum or an annuitized amount for the rest of your life. On that matter, all pensions are just giant annuities. Even Social Security is a giant annuity! Like your pension or your Social Security, once you pick or trigger your annuitized payment from your FIA, your annuity income is set for life. You'll never have to manage this money as you do a stock market account or a rental property.

An issuing insurance company guarantees your income for life just as the federal government guarantees your Social Security benefit. I give my clients options from highly rated insurance companies that have usually been around for more than a hundred years or longer. They are insured in a similar way to how the Federal Deposit Insurance Corporation (FDIC) insures your bank account, with the amount varying according to the state rules where you wrote the contract. Depending on the state, this can mean that, with an insurance-company-issued fixed index annuity, you're often insured at or more than you are with the US government. And if that's not enough, these insurance companies also are insured by other insurance companies. Because even though they have their own assets backing their promises, they also buy reinsurance on themselves to ensure they can still meet all their obligations to you if they do suffer a catastrophic loss.

Another reason the guarantees are so strong from insurance companies is the fact that they are even more regulated than banks are. A bank's typical reserve requirement is 10 percent of the deposit, while the life insurance company that is holding your annuity would more likely have 80-100 percent of your money in reserve. This is huge! If you are looking for safety and guarantees, an annuity can be one of your best options.

That's why when you are looking to reduce or eliminate risk to your financial accounts, look for institutions that provide guarantees, and then find out what those guarantees are backed up with. Guarantees are only as strong as the backing financial institution is, which is why I focus on highly rated insurance companies with huge reserve requirements.

The biggest way I help you manage risk is either to reduce it or eliminate it by transferring the risk to someone else—like an insurance company. By investing money into fixed index annuities, you *eliminate market risk*. Your annuity value goes up when the market goes up. But when the market declines, you retain your prior gains. If the market's going down right now, the worst that can happen to you is that your account won't earn anything during the crediting period. Your valuation will just be flat, staying where it was when the market slump began. This is a big advantage because you won't have to try and claw back all the losses like everyone else—because you don't have any.

In the stock market, it can take five to seven years after a major slump just to get your stock portfolio back to breakeven. Managing risk, especially five to ten years from retirement, is crucial. You manage risk by getting most or all of your nest egg out of the market. If you don't, it will change your entire retirement picture.

When you are looking at how to set up guaranteed income for life, your focus is on getting the most income every month or year from the fixed index annuity you choose and not losing a dime of the money you put into the annuity due to market fluctuation.

You Have a Lot of Choices

I would say there are over 200 different fixed index annuities. While I would never show a client so many, I still think it's important you know how much is out there.

I show this to my clients visually with several options. There are many advisors who will pitch only one or two annuities because they are either captive agents or they are being tempted by large commissions from certain carriers. This, of course, presents a conflict of interest that many advisors won't disclose. When I show annuity options to my clients, I present twenty or thirty of the top fixed index annuities, all of which are A-rated. The annuities sell themselves. I don't need to push a client into a particular one. I focus on educating them on the pros and cons of each one and recommending the one that best fits their needs.

I was showing the differences in various A-rated annuities to one of my clients recently. One annuity was from a company that had been around for 175 years. We looked at the income payout on that option as well as other benefits. Then I showed him another one from a different company where his payout was 20 percent higher. This was also a highly rated company. Sure, the indexes were a little bit more flexible in the first company, but the actual income was much higher in the second carrier. Since the most important thing to this client was to have the highest income from an A-rated company, he saw a clear choice.

Consider events affecting the economy for the past two centuries, such as the Great Depression, wars, financial markets' ups and downs, government shifts and changes, and COVID-19. Insurance companies have weathered such storms with sound planning for 100 to 200 years and have remained highly rated as a result. They've never broken a promise. When you're investing your money in a company that's been around safely for a long time, you're putting yourself in a risk-free, guaranteed income bucket.

Fees and Downsides

The only risk in a fixed index annuity is the 0 percent floor pertaining to the index. Say the index loses 20 percent. You're guaranteed to lose zero if the floor is zero. The only cost to you for your annuity is the annual charge for the guaranteed income rider (or zero if you did not select an income rider when purchasing the contract). Typically, fixed index annuities, that focus on high guaranteed income streams, charge roughly 1 percent annually (some are as high as 2 percent). Your worst-case scenario is that you are in a fixed index annuity with a 0 percent floor as part of the contract. If the index suffers and goes down 20 percent, you already know your floor, and you're not losing a dime due to market fluctuations. However, don't forget the insurance company is still spending money to protect your account as well as your guaranteed income contract. You'll probably see $99,000 in the annuity instead of $100,000 because of that 1 percent charge. This will not, however, affect the guaranteed income you are entitled to within the contract. Even if the index never experienced growth for 20 years and your account was eaten away by fees, your guaranteed income would never go away.

Too many of the people I talk with get so hung up by the fees or what the index is earning that they forget the primary reason they purchased the annuity: guaranteed income for life.

Investment Vehicles for Annuities

The majority of people I speak with have traditional tax-deferred retirement accounts, such as a tax-deferred 401(k), 403(b), TSP, individual retirement account (IRA), or similar. So, when thinking about funding an annuity for guaranteed income, you will generally transfer from one tax-deferred account to another one. A common method at retirement is to transfer from a traditional 401(k) to a traditional IRA. At this point, you may choose to invest into an annuity inside that new IRA. If the money for the annuity is coming from cash savings, stock, or another account, it is known as nonqualified money (meaning that it is not subject to Internal Revenue Service (IRS) rules for qualified retirement accounts like a 401(k), IRA, etc.).

If you want to eliminate income taxes during retirement, then a popular option is to convert your traditional 401(k), 403(b), or IRA (or similar) into a Roth account. The advantages are when you start taking income later from your newly converted Roth account, you won't be subject to the current income tax rate (does anyone believe taxes will go down?), nor will you be subject to RMDs (required minimum distributions).

Different Scenarios for Setting Up Your Annuity

Timing can be critical.

There isn't necessarily a right or wrong time to make this investment. However, there are three situations where purchasing one will make the most sense:

1. **When you're saving for retirement.** If you're already putting the maximum into other retirement funds, then a fixed indexed annuity may be an ideal investment for you. This will add some more cushion to your retirement savings, especially since it's tax-deferred.

2. **When you aren't strapped for cash.** If you're comfortable in your current situation and don't expect the need to invest the money, then a fixed annuity may be ideal for you. As long as you don't need the money before you turn 59½ (unless it's unqualified money), then the investment can shape up to be a great way to maximize your retirement income.

3. **When your current investment account won't cover you.** Ideally, you'll never outlive your retirement fund. You want your money to comfortably cover you for the rest of your life so you're free to enjoy retirement. Annuities provide the comfort of a steady income for

life, even if you live to be over one hundred years old. In this day and age, becoming a centenarian is much more common.

There are different ways to fund an annuity. You can fund it upfront with a one-time lump sum contribution or contribute on a monthly, quarterly, or annual basis, depending on your account.

It's the compounding effect of time that really makes the difference here.

Let's say that at age thirty you have half a million dollars saved. By funding an annuity at that time, you give that money more time to grow to a more significant amount. Twenty years later, when you start taking out that guaranteed income, it will be considerable.

Alternatively, at age thirty, you learn about annuities and decide to contribute to one every single month. This can be done inside of an IRA or 401(k), but you'll need to ask a professional how to set it up properly.

A lot of people don't have piles of cash when they're in their thirties but they do in their fifties and sixties. If they are planning to retire in a few years, they need a way to protect their money before retirement. If they're also sick of the stock market and worried about the safety of their stock portfolio, they need a solution to protect it and still provide growth in the interim. Ultimately, they want to make sure they can turn on a guaranteed stream of income later.

So, at whatever age you come into it, annuities might be part of your solution.

Indexes and Caps

When you set up your fixed index annuity, usually its best to put your money in indexes with very high or zero "caps." Having an index cap will mean there is a limit to what the upside profits or gains can be in your account. With the zero percent protected floor and a high or zero cap, you are protected from loss and assured of maximizing all potential gains.

Now let's talk about market risk and income factors associated with a fixed index annuity.

We all love growth in these accounts, but if the market goes down for twenty years, you need to know that you are protected and your income stream continues to flow to you – even if your account balance goes to zero. If the stock market goes away (as the very worst-case scenario, of course) and you're not making any money at all, your income stream still never stops. This is why paying for a guaranteed income rider is so beneficial.

Suppose your whole focus is income. Let's say you have an account with $100,000 giving you a guaranteed income of $7,000 a year. You could have ten or fifteen years when the market doesn't make any money at all, and your account balance could lose value during that time due to the annual payment of fees and the income you turned on. Yet, you could potentially withdraw in annuity payments three times the amount you put in that investment. For instance, you might take $300,000 in total income from your $100,000 annuity over your retirement. The fact is that the annuity continues to pay you regardless of how long you live or if your account value goes to zero early in the contract.

By choosing to invest in a fixed index annuity, you're not just managing, but eliminating the risk of running out of income. No matter what the market does, your income stream never stops. And that's the most important thing as far as managing risk.

The main thing to remember for fixed index annuities is that you are basically purchasing a guaranteed pension when investing in an annuity. You are essentially transferring the risk of running out of income to the insurance company before you run out of life.

In fixed index annuities, principal protection is the most important, then income, then growth.

Even when the market drops, the worst thing that happens to people with fixed index annuities accounts is their account goes flat. These accounts don't lose a dime while the overall market loses potentially trillions. When everyone else is clawing back their losses over four or more years after that, those fixed index annuity accounts are all going up in value *from their previous high values* because they only have upsides. They're all protected from downsides. Every credited gain inside a fixed index annuity is a new low-water mark. It only goes up from there!

With such investments (especially those made early, where you contribute money to the annuity every month), you're stairstepping your way to higher wealth versus riding the market rollercoaster's ups and downs. It's just a smoother ride. These fixed index accounts are guaranteed against any type of loss due to market fluctuations because of how they are structured.

When you realize the degree of risk to your stock portfolio, for example, you might want to convert some of those assets into annuities that pay out much more to you without the management headache and risk of loss. There's no guarantee with stocks. They may or may not be worth more in ten or twenty years. With your annuity, though, you get to keep all gains you earn. There's no management to a fixed index annuity as with an actively managed stock portfolio. Yes, over time, the stock market has proved that its value goes up, but as you age, do you want to deal with the management involved or be free of the stress and worry that comes with it?

I'm not saying to dump your whole stock portfolio— not at all. It depends on your goals and intentions. If you want to leave these assets as a legacy to your heirs, by all means, do so! My only point with a traditionally managed stock account is that there's no guarantee of what income it will be able to provide you during your retirement.

The real risk is not having enough money in your later years when you need it the most. It might make sense to come talk to me about the fixed index annuity solution and what it might be able to provide you. My door is always open, and I won't try to sell you anything either!

Another aspect of risk to avoid? The money you put in your fixed index annuity should never be the cash you might need for meeting emergency expenses in the foreseeable future. It needs to be money that's set aside to give you income upon retirement for the rest of your life. This means you need to set aside some amount of savings that you can access in case of an immediate need. No one in this business wants you to be short of ready cash in an emergency. Annuity companies also require that you have ample savings over what you are using to fund your annuity.

Is an Annuity Right for You?

Social Security, IRAs, and pensions don't always have you covered. A fixed index annuity can supplement the gaps in your retirement fund.

Annuities make a good retirement investment because you have the guarantee of a monthly income that you might not otherwise receive, depending on your financial situation. You will receive this money each month for the rest of your life regardless of market conditions.

With a fixed annuity, you have a periodic flow of income that never stops. This can be purchased in a lump sum, which immediately generates income if desired. There are also a variety of payout options offered by your chosen insurance carrier. The structure of this investment is determined by the contract set with your insurance carrier. Typically, the younger you are when you choose to receive the benefits, the lower your monthly income payments will be. However, each company determines its payment schedule based on the individual's expected mortality rate and the carrier's expected earnings. Just remember, you're purchasing the guarantee of a fixed lifetime income as well as complete safety of your capital.

Looking Out for You

I'm licensed to create these annuity solutions for my clients, but I don't recommend a fixed index annuity solution to everyone. With each client who believes this is his or her retirement funding solution, I look closely at their overall financial situation with them.

First, you have to have decent savings or investments—a fair amount of cash you can invest into these vehicles. Second, you need to have enough available cash savings (in addition to what you put into the annuity) to cover any emergencies requiring immediate cash. Third, it's my job to make sure this type of investment is suitable for you and your circumstances. If not, I won't set it up for you but instead look at other solutions with you.

Amount Invested?

I recommend my clients invest at least $100,000, which is the average sum to receive a viable amount of guaranteed income later; the average annuity is around $250,000. However, I've seen $1–$5 million invested in these annuities.

Theodore Manages Risk

Theodore contacted me with goals of (1) no more losses to his account due to market fluctuations and (2) a steady stream of income for retirement he wanted to trigger one year from the day he came to see me.

When he came to me for help, he was losing money in his account; in fact, it was down nearly $200,000 before he contacted me. It was not his only asset. He had about $500,000 in home equity plus about the same amount sitting in another account due to an inheritance from his parents.

His goal was that in one year, when he retired, he wanted at least $60,000 a year in guaranteed retirement income. He had Social Security, but like most people, that amount fell short of his income goal. After reviewing his options, he decided to roll $500,000 into a fixed index annuity which would make up the income gap he would experience. The annuity would provide $36,000 a year for life, plus a good rate of return.

We probably looked at twenty annuities. As I am always careful to point out to all my clients, I showed Theodore the differences between the different annuity options regarding the monthly guaranteed income each one provided. For instance, even though the investment amount was $500,000, one annuity might pay significantly more than another because of different benefits or riders offered by that carrier. That $500,000 in one account might provide $25,000 in annual income but have a lower surrender charge schedule, whereas the second option would provide $36,000 in annual income but not have as easy access to the principal.

Theodore chose one providing decent growth and the highest amount of income; it was with a company that was 175 years old. He felt confident about his selection after looking at the different options.

Theodore knew his assets were of great value, but he also knew that what he really needed was a sustainable stream of income when he retired. Will he invest his other $500,000 inheritance in the markets? Perhaps. He can do so knowing he has enough guaranteed, predictable income for the rest of his life from the annuity investment and his Social Security.

You might be saying, "But John, what if I don't have a large asset base like Theodore has? Is an annuity still a possible option?" In other words, am I able to write a fixed annuity contract for your $50,000 that's sitting in a bank? The answer is yes. It might only give you

$300–$400 per month. But you can still count on it for life, which is important for many people. So, yes, we can—especially if you already have sufficient income from a pension and Social Security, and the investable assets are not emergency funds for you.

I just rolled $135,000 into a fixed index annuity for another client; this came straight from his old 401k account. He understands if he waits two years to start taking his money, he'll get an income stream for life at $13,000 a year. That is great for him as an addition to his Social Security and pension!

It's important to me to make sure it's the best thing for you. My clients are looking at *all* of their income sources with me—pensions, Social Security, cash, passive income, and other noncash assets, like real estate. I gather this information to see if you have an income gap either now or in the future. And if you do, we can often close that income gap with an annuity—a solution with a guarantee that you will never outlive the income.

A case in point is Rodrigo.

A Policeman Makes Up for Market Losses and Maximizes Social Security

Rodrigo came to me with two main concerns. He is sixty-four years old and retired from the police department after thirty-three years of service. Right now, his money is in a state-sponsored deferred compensation plan.

The state's plan does not give him any opportunity to get out of the market or reduce his risk. All they gave him were different types of mutual funds, but there were no safe funds anywhere in the plan. He wanted to move his money into safe funds because his account had gone down quite a bit from the 2022 market downturn. Every quarter he keeps on looking at losses, and he's so frustrated. At one point, he had $165,000 in the account.

He decided to move $135,000 into a fixed index annuity after losing roughly $30,000 in the market. In this case, the carrier was also offering a 10 percent premium bonus paying him an immediate $13,500. The contract bonus is a credit the annuity company will put into his account as a thank-you, but in his case, it helps him make up for some of his losses.

He also has a pension providing him $4,200 per month. This fixed index annuity will give him an additional $1,100 per month. With the extra income coming in from his annuity, he can wait longer to trigger his Social Security benefit and get paid out much more. While he can afford to wait until age seventy, he now has more freedom to take it early or defer it for a higher benefit later.

For a joint payout option, when he dies, the beneficiary of his fixed index annuity (often a spouse) can decide to take the lump sum or continue the income as before. So, the income will not decrease upon his death like it would with Social Security or with a pension.

Do It Yourself?

This is not a do-it-yourself investment solution. It is different from going into your online trading account and buying 150 shares of stock. Insurance companies won't allow you to buy an annuity by yourself. You have to consult with a professional who looks at your whole situation to make sure it is in your best interest. A professional like me looks at the suitability of the investment for you according to your financial situation. I also use best practices to look for something that is in your best interest while avoiding any conflicts of interest, such as a commission incentive offered by a particular carrier to recommend their annuity over another one that might benefit you more. While I can certainly set up any annuity for you, my licensing and training require me to look at your financial picture to know what to present to you to best fit your needs and situation.

In Summary: The Benefits of a Fixed Index Annuity

While this is not a do-it-yourself investment solution, the benefits of consulting with an advisor and setting up fixed index annuities are numerous.

By putting money into fixed index annuities, you *eliminate market risk*. Your annuity value goes up when the market goes up. But when the market declines, you retain your prior gains. When the market rises again, you pick up where you left off and keep on earning— while others invested in stocks are still waiting to catch back up to their breakeven point.

Income tax on annuities is deferred, meaning you are not taxed on the interest your money earns while it remains under the contract of the annuity. The money is compounded each year without a tax bill, allowing you to use every penny you've saved to generate a larger investment as opposed to what you would lose with alternative taxable investments.

One of the biggest advantages of purchasing fixed index annuities is the guaranteed income. This type of guaranteed income can only come from insurance company-issued annuities with lifetime contractual income payments.

Unlike other tax-deferred qualified retirement accounts, your contributions could have no annual contribution limits. This makes investing additional money for retirement easier, which is especially helpful when you're close to retiring but need a little push to catch up with your retirement income goals.

Your advisor should help you select an A-rated insurance company for your fixed index annuity investment. Remember, such companies have weathered storms in the economy for well over a century and have to meet high standards to ensure they can pay out your guaranteed retirement income no matter how long you live.

The income annuity contract is for whenever you decide to retire and designed to be there for however long you need the money. Once triggered, the amount of your monthly income is guaranteed for life. You cannot outlive this income!

Maximizing Social Security

3

IF YOU READ THE TITLE OF THIS CHAPTER, you might be saying, "John, the Social Security Administration will only give me what I qualified for. *They* tell me how much it is. I take what I can get. So how can I 'maximize' what is a fixed amount?"

Let's talk about the age you take your benefit amount. This is called the Primary Insurance Amount (PIA). The reason why the word *insurance* is in there is because it is just a giant annuity! The earliest age to take your PIA is age sixty-two for anyone who has worked and qualified for it; this is also the common age people turn on their benefit. At sixty-two, however, you get 30 percent *less* for the rest of your life than you would get at your "full" retirement age—assuming your full retirement age (FRA) is sixty-seven. Taking your FRA benefit then gives you 100 percent of the benefit. The "full" age usually is either sixty-six or sixty-seven, depending on when you were born. (See the ssa.gov website for your FRA age).

But if you wait until age seventy, the administration gives you another 8 percent per year on top of your full retirement benefit amount! This is an additional 24 percent if your FRA is sixty-seven, and it's the maximum amount the administration will ever pay out to you.

By waiting until seventy to start your benefit, you can perhaps get $3,100 per month for the rest of your life versus $2,500 per month at age sixty-seven. You may like that idea, but maybe you don't want to actually work until age seventy! You may want to retire earlier—maybe even *much* earlier.

So, how can you bridge that income gap of several years? What are you going to use to pay yourself between the day you decide to retire to age seventy (assuming you will not be taking Social security income)?

I first told you about fixed index annuities, so you could easily see how they can help you maximize your Social Security benefit if you were to turn on the lifetime income amounts earlier than when you wanted to start taking your Social Security benefit. When done properly, there are *annuity strategies* that will allow you to fund your retirement while you wait until age seventy to claim that top Social Security benefit amount, thereby allowing you to *maximize* your Social Security payout at age seventy.

Using Annuities to Fund the Income Gap

Let's say your Social Security retirement benefit will pay out $1,400 per month for life if you take your benefit at age sixty-two. It rises to $2,000 per month if you can wait until your full retirement age of sixty-seven. If you wait until age seventy to trigger your payments, the administration increases your full amount by 8 percent a year for three years, a total increase of 24 percent. In this example, you'd get $2,480 per month at age seventy. In other words, to *maximize your Social Security benefit,* you need a way to pay the bills until age seventy.

What does that look like for my clients making different retirement decisions? Let's look at some strategies I've discussed with clients retiring at different ages but wishing to maximize their Social Security.

The first scenario is that you take money, maybe $300,000 or $400,000, sitting in one of your accounts (whether a bank or trading account or a 401(k) account) and use it to fund an annuity. You would choose an annuity that will give you a guaranteed payout to fund your lifestyle starting today and for the rest of your life. This payout also gives you the minimum income needed to retire now without taking an early and reduced Social Security benefit. At seventy, you trigger your maximum Social Security benefit.

Even choosing to fund an annuity to give you income starting at sixty-two to match your age sixty-two

Social Security benefit would work. That might be all you need.

In a second scenario, you might be in your mid-fifties and already know you want to take your reduced Social Security benefit right at age sixty-two. For whatever reason, you are not willing to wait until your full retirement age, nor age seventy for your maximum benefit. Should you take your Social Security benefit at age sixty-two? Let me first be clear that it is a personal decision based on your life circumstances, family longevity, and financial situation. I would normally say *not* to take it at that age if you want to maximize your benefit, but the decision is naturally yours to make.

How do you maximize your income in this second scenario? You fund an annuity as early as you can, so it will defer long enough to start paying out an income high enough to you at age sixty-two. You will then have the annuity income in addition to your reduced Social Security benefit at age sixty-two. Continuing your planning, you fund a second annuity that you defer longer to start paying out to you later and at a higher amount, for example, at age sixty-seven. Now you have your Social Security income, the first annuity income, and the second annuity, which is currently paying you for life. Your total income is now greater from age sixty-seven and for the rest of your life.

In a third scenario to maximize your Social Security, you decide to retire at age sixty. At sixty, you know you cannot yet take your benefit. You know that when you take your Social Security benefit at sixty-two, it will be, for example, $1,600 per month. In this example, you're not willing to annuitize your benefit at that early, lower income level. You will need a solution to create income not only between the ages of sixty and sixty-two, but also between the ages of sixty and seventy so you can afford to wait to receive your maximum Social Security. This can likewise be a situation where one or more annuities *start paying you income in different years*.

Funding one annuity to start paying you income when you retire early can allow you to wait until your full retirement age or age seventy before triggering your *maximized* Social Security benefit. Funding two or more annuities whose start dates are staggered to fund your retirement is what we call *laddering annuities* and is a strategy that helps your income increase over time.

Closing the Retirement Income Gap

Melanie is from Kentucky and, at age sixty, works as a nurse for the Veterans Administration (VA) health care system. She wants to retire at sixty-seven. She loves hanging out with her kids and grandkids, and barbecuing. She wants to have the freedom to do that when she retires without worrying about money.

If she doesn't do anything, her Social Security will provide $25,836 per year, on top of her VA pension which will be $7,200 per year. She wants her income to be at least $50,000. So, her gap is about $17,000 annually. I set her up with a fixed index annuity that would more than fill the income gap; in fact, it will give her another $18,630 seven years from now. By investing into the annuity at sixty, it will give her $18,630 per year at age sixty-seven and for the rest of her life. She invested $200,000 to achieve this.

Melanie was super nervous to do this, by the way. She really didn't want to make mistakes with what she felt was a very small nest egg. So, there was a lot of reassuring. And the fact that she was rolling the money into an A-rated company that has been in existence since 1848 helped reassure her. I understood her position; the $200,000 was her life savings. She didn't want to lose a dime of it.

Another of my clients wishes to stop working at sixty-two. However, he's decided he doesn't want to take the lower benefits from Social Security. Instead, he'll buy an annuity with some of his savings that will pay a guaranteed income for the rest of his life and use the income to fund his lifestyle until he reaches sixty-seven or maybe even seventy. At his chosen age, he'll apply for Social Security benefits, which are not only much higher but are locked in for life at a higher amount.

My client Rodrigo, who I mentioned earlier, is turning his $135,000 savings of today into a $13,000 per year income stream in retirement, thanks to an annuity.

Many of my clients see the beauty of this additional stream of guaranteed income, and they fund these annuities starting in their late forties to early fifties. They don't activate it or touch it until retirement. The annuity sits, accruing in value while protecting against market risk. The annuity payout deferment time period is important to know, as your guaranteed payout will be higher the longer you wait to trigger it (also known as "annuitizing" it or activating the guaranteed lifetime income rider). A married couple who are both schoolteachers illustrate this.

Teachers Protect Their Nest Egg

Daniella and her husband, James, are schoolteachers who came to me looking for ways to diversify and protect their nest egg through smarter investments.

Because they are teachers, they are on a defined benefit pension plan. They'll get a pension along with their Social Security, but they have another fifteen years until their retirement. They realized there would be a significant income gap at retirement, even after their Social Security benefit and pension payout. They wanted to do their financial restructuring early, knowing these annuity accounts would be protected for those fifteen years, but would also grow. They also knew they would have more guaranteed income streams by doing this.

The combined Social Security income for both James and Daniella would be $42,000, which was not enough even with their small pension. They decided to invest into two annuities providing another $31,000 in income, raising their annual retirement income to almost $100,000.

How did they fund these annuities?

Daniella and James had IRAs holding only mutual funds. They both transferred their money out of them just before the market dropped in March 2022. Daniella transferred $50,000, while James transferred $75,000. They created new IRAs with their chosen insurance company, which would be the new fiduciary of their IRAs. Instead of putting mutual funds in them as was the case with their first IRA, they both purchased fixed index annuities inside them with guaranteed income riders attached.

Note that if people transfer their money from their 401(k) at retirement and want to keep it in tax-deferred status, it must always be transferred to an IRA. They can either transfer it to an IRA that will continue to hold stocks, bonds, and mutual funds, or they can transfer it to an IRA *held at an insurance company* (not many people know about this option) and fill it with fixed index products, like annuities, that provide income. Daniella and James felt secure about this new safe money investment, and they were confident the income stream would be enough for their retirement.

There are annuity payout options you can discuss with me to fit your needs. Perhaps an annuity would give you $1,000 per month if you trigger it at age sixty-two, but if you wait five more years, it will give you $2,000 per month. Again, if you wait eight years instead of five, it will give you $3,000 per month. Letting time do its magic for you to accumulate value is the key here; you need to determine how long you are willing to wait in order to calculate the guaranteed monthly income that an annuity can provide.

Laddering a Sum of $600,000

I told you in a prior section that a third option for funding your retirement was *laddering annuities.*

There is a laddering solution to help you not only wait several more years so you maximize your Social Security benefit, but also fight future inflationary effects on your purchase power.

How does that look? What do the numbers look like? In this example, we'll say you're sixty-five and have $600,000 to invest. Since you want your income to keep rising as you age, you might want to consider laddering your annuity contracts. Laddering involves purchasing more than one annuity, and then triggering the income at different dates with each annuity. So for this example, we'll assume you invest your full $600,000 by purchasing three different annuities at the same time, each one for $200,000.

How would it look?

Your *first annuity* provides you with $15,000 per year from the $200,000 invested if you trigger it right away.

You know you'll need more than that as you age (even with your pension and Social Security).

You, therefore, buy a _second annuity_ at the same time, also for $200,000, but you defer starting the monthly payments for five years. In five years, the annuity value rises and will give you $21,000 a year for life.

Likewise, at the same time, you buy a _third annuity_ with your last $200,000. You intend to let it grow without starting monthly payments to you until it provides you an additional $31,000 per year guaranteed for life.

With your initial $600,000, you have laddered three annuities that, when the third one is annuitized, provide $67,000 per year on top of your pension and Social Security. By staggering the start date of each one, you ensure income for life to keep up with inflation (and probably a lot more).

The exact values are hard for an individual to calculate. I must repeat: This is not a do-it-yourself strategy. I help most of my clients understand how much income they can expect by waiting a certain number of years to trigger it. Also, different annuities work better for longer income deferral times. If this is a strategy that appeals to you, speak to me to see how much your current nest egg can earn for you in different annuity and wait-time scenarios.

Laddering annuities is a wise strategy when you are seeking guaranteed income for life that will keep up with the rising costs of living. If you need $60,000 a year now but you are aware that in ten years your buying power will be reduced due to inflation, you think ahead by laddering. You'll say, "I'll need $70,000 per year ten years from now; then another ten years later, I'll need $80,000." Laddering annuities allows you to achieve more income over time, in addition to the huge benefit of maximizing your Social Security by being able to wait longer to take it.

With laddering, you're planning your future income. You can always turn on these annuity start dates earlier or wait longer. These contracts are flexible, and the timing is up to you. You can turn on the income when you need it and as inflation rises, you will continue to be able to meet your income needs.

To ladder annuities with your saved cash, you can invest in such a strategy at any age. The sooner you invest the better, naturally, so the annuity's value has time to increase before you trigger the regular income payments. These income payments from the annuity can also help you wait for your maximum Social Security benefit later. This strategy can work for you if you start in your forties and even in your sixties and have not yet triggered your Social Security benefits. You should, at whatever age, consult with me. I'll be happy to run the numbers for you.

Again, this laddering strategy is valuable for someone who does not need social security and just wants to keep up with inflation. It also works for someone who has *not* yet activated their Social Security and wants to get the maximum payout, but still retire earlier. If this is your case, you should meet with someone to go over your situation and see what you can do with an annuity laddering strategy. First, you should go to www. ssa.gov and register for an account so you can see exactly what your benefit payout would be at each age you might take it.

In the following two graphic illustrations, John Doe and Jane Doe use annuities in ways you might find useful.

In Jane's case, her intention was to have enough income from the annuities that she could wait until age seventy to start her Social Security, John's thinking was a bit different. He decided to take his Social Security at his full benefit age of sixty-six and use laddering to maximize his overall income as he grows older.

In both cases, you see how income maximization in retirement can occur through laddering strategies.

Jane Doe: Social Security Maximization

I've included a table below showing an annuity investment available for Jane Doe. She has a cash amount of $500,000 to invest in an annuity to give her income starting at age sixty for as long as she lives. Having this annuity income will allow her to wait until age seventy to take her Social Security benefits, and thus maximize the amount she receives.

From age seventy, her income of $57,850 is comprised of her annuity income of $30,250 (enough for her costs of living since she has no debt) and her Social Security benefit of $27,600. These combined incomes are guaranteed for as long as she lives.

Jane feels she is going to live into her late nineties and wants to retire at age sixty. Because she believes in her longevity, she wants to create the most income possible. This plan works for her. Having no debt allows her to live the same lifestyle right away, even with less money than her current salary.

ANNUAL INCOME PLANNER Social Security Maximization for Jane Doe Desired Annual Income: $30,000						
Year	Age	Current Job	$500K Annuity	Social Security	Total Annual Income	Surplus Income
0	59	$50,000.00	$0.00	$0.00	$50,000.00	$20,000.00
1	60	$0.00	$30,250.00	$0.00	$30,250.00	$250.00
2	61	$0.00	$30,250.00	$0.00	$30,250.00	$250.00
3	62	$0.00	$30,250.00	$0.00	$30,250.00	$250.00
4	63	$0.00	$30,250.00	$0.00	$30,250.00	$250.00
5	64	$0.00	$30,250.00	$0.00	$30,250.00	$250.00
6	65	$0.00	$30,250.00	$0.00	$30,250.00	$250.00
7	66	$0.00	$30,250.00	$0.00	$30,250.00	$250.00
8	67	$0.00	$30,250.00	$0.00	$30,250.00	$250.00
9	68	$0.00	$30,250.00	$0.00	$30,250.00	$250.00
10	69	$0.00	$30,250.00	$0.00	$30,250.00	$250.00
11	70	$0.00	$30,250.00	$27,600.00	$57,850.00	$27,850.00
12	71	$0.00	$30,250.00	$28,014.00	$58,264.00	$28,264.00
13	72	$0.00	$30,250.00	$28,434.21	$58,684.21	$28,684.21

					Total	
Year	Age	Current Job	$500K Annuity	Social Security	Annual Income	Surplus Income
14	73	$0.00	$30,250.00	$28,860.72	$59,110.72	$29,110.72
15	74	$0.00	$30,250.00	$29,293.63	$59,543.63	$29,543.63
16	75	$0.00	$30,250.00	$29,733.03	$59,983.03	$29,983.03
17	76	$0.00	$30,250.00	$30,179.03	$60,429.03	$30,429.03
18	77	$0.00	$30,250.00	$30,631.72	$60,881.72	$30,881.72
19	78	$0.00	$30,250.00	$31,091.20	$61,341.20	$31,341.20
20	79	$0.00	$30,250.00	$31,557.57	$61,807.57	$31,807.57
21	80	$0.00	$30,250.00	$32,030.93	$62,280.93	$32,280.93
22	81	$0.00	$30,250.00	$32,511.39	$62,761.39	$32,761.39
23	82	$0.00	$30,250.00	$32,999.06	$63,249.06	$33,249.06
24	83	$0.00	$30,250.00	$33,494.05	$63,744.05	$33,494.05
25	84	$0.00	$30,250.00	$33,996.46	$64,246.46	$34,246.46

ANNUAL INCOME PLANNER
Social Security Maximization for Jane Doe
Desired Annual Income: $30,000

John Doe: Income Laddering Annuities

John Doe wants more income as time passes while taking his Social Security at his full age, so he has chosen to purchase three annuities right now. He has $600,000 and will structure three $200,000 annuities.

The chart below does not show the *income growth* of each annuity over time as he waits to trigger the income. However, his second annuity grows in value for ten years, and the third grows over twenty years with the effect of producing a higher income for him once he annuitizes each of them.

He will retire at his full retirement age of sixty-six one year from now and start his Social Security benefit at that age. He chose not to wait until age seventy as Jane Doe did. At that same age, he will start taking income from his first annuity. His income from Social Security and the first annuity comes to $51,698 per year. Both incomes are guaranteed for life.

In ten years, he will start the lifetime income payouts from his second annuity. Not only has the value of the second annuity grown over the ten years, but due to the Cost of Living Adjustments (COLA), his Social Security at that time will be about $4,800 more than it was ten years earlier or $38,875.26 per year. His income from all guaranteed sources is thus increased from the initial $51,698 to $87,430.26.

In twenty years, he will then start the lifetime income payouts from his third annuity, which is shown coming in on top of the continuing (and again increased) Social Security and the first and second annuity incomes. His total income that year rises to $137,396.33.

Note that while Social Security gets periodic cost of living adjustments, his annuities do not. Once annuitized, the payout remains at the same amount for their duration. There are annuities that provide increasing income each year, but are not shown in this illustration (typically increasing annuities grow much slower than inflation does).

By doing this annuity laddering, he is able to count on higher income as he gets older; he could have triggered his annuities at earlier years for different payout results. He has more income to mitigate and pay the increased out-of-pocket costs for his potential health care and long-term care if needed. Of course, he can also fund any other bucket list desires that might cost more money.

ANNUAL INCOME PLANNER
Annuity Laddering Strategy for John Doe
Desired Annual Income: $50,000

Year	Age	Current Job	Social Security	1st Annuity	2nd Annuity	3rd Annuity	Total Annual Income	Surplus Income
0	65	$80,000.00	$0.00	$0.00	$0.00	$0.00	$80,000.00	$30,000.00
1	66	$0.00	$34,000.00	$17,698.00	$0.00	$0.00	$51,698.00	$1,698.00
2	67	$0.00	$34,510.00	$17,698.00	$0.00	$0.00	$52,208.00	$2,208.00
3	68	$0.00	$35,027.65	$17,698.00	$0.00	$0.00	$52,725.65	$2,725.65
4	69	$0.00	$35,553.06	$17,698.00	$0.00	$0.00	$53,251.06	$3,251.06
5	70	$0.00	$36,086.36	$17,698.00	$0.00	$0.00	$53,784.36	$3,784.36
6	71	$0.00	$36,627.66	$17,698.00	$0.00	$0.00	$54,325.66	$4,325.66
7	72	$0.00	$37,177.07	$17,698.00	$0.00	$0.00	$54,875.07	$4,875.07
8	73	$0.00	$37,734.73	$17,698.00	$0.00	$0.00	$55,432.73	$5,432.73
9	74	$0.00	$38,300.75	$17,698.00	$0.00	$0.00	$55,998.75	$5,998.75
10	75	$0.00	$38,875.26	$17,698.00	$30,857.00	$0.00	$87,430.26	$37,430.26
11	76	$0.00	$39,458.39	$17,698.00	$30,857.00	$0.00	$88,013.39	$38,013.39
12	77	$0.00	$40,050.27	$17,698.00	$30,857.00	$0.00	$88,605.27	$38,605.27
13	78	$0.00	$40,651.02	$17,698.00	$30,857.00	$0.00	$89,206.02	$39,206.02
14	79	$0.00	$41,260.79	$17,698.00	$30,857.00	$0.00	$89,815.79	$39,815.79
15	80	$0.00	$41,879.70	$17,698.00	$30,857.00	$0.00	$90,434.70	$40,434.70
16	81	$0.00	$42,507.90	$17,698.00	$30,857.00	$0.00	$91,062.90	$41,062.90
17	82	$0.00	$43,145.52	$17,698.00	$30,857.00	$0.00	$91,700.52	$41,700.52
18	83	$0.00	$43,792.70	$17,698.00	$30,857.00	$0.00	$92,347.70	$42,347.70
19	84	$0.00	$44,449.59	$17,698.00	$30,857.00	$0.00	$93,004.59	$43,004.59
20	85	$0.00	$45,116.33	$17,698.00	$30,857.00	$43,725.00	$137,396.33	$87,396.33
21	86	$0.00	$45,793.07	$17,698.00	$30,857.00	$43,725.00	$138,073.07	$88,073.07
22	87	$0.00	$46,479.97	$17,698.00	$30,857.00	$43,725.00	$138,759.97	$88,759.97
23	88	$0.00	$47,177.17	$17,698.00	$30,857.00	$43,725.00	$139,457.17	$89,457.17
24	89	$0.00	$47,884.83	$17,698.00	$30,857.00	$43,725.00	$140,164.83	$90,164.83

4
Tax-Free Retirement Accounts (TFRA)

I NOW WANT TO SPEAK TO YOU about another vehicle that has been used by the rich for quite a while. It can be set up for anyone, but has been used mainly by very affluent individuals, families, and banks, solely because no one else is really talking about it! It is called the tax-free retirement account (TFRA).

A TFRA is a cash-value life insurance policy categorized as IRS Tax Code Section 7702. As you now know, I am licensed to present insurance products to clients from all insurance companies in the country. In other words, I don't represent companies. I represent you and your best interests. Keep in mind that there are hundreds of products; Don't worry, I'm well versed in the best ones to present to you! I've looked through hundreds of options for clients so I can find a perfect match for tax-free income needs, growth expectations, and nest egg protection.

After being exposed to these for over twenty years, I can say the TFRA is one of the best ways to build tax-free wealth while avoiding market losses. You basically leverage the rules and laws of life insurance to create tax-free income at retirement. Not tax-*deferred*, but tax-*free*.

For this, you're utilizing an *indexed universal life policy* or IUL that is tied to an external index. It might be the S&P 500 index, for instance. It's very similar to an annuity; if the market is going up, you reap those gains in your TFRA. And then, like the fixed index annuity we discussed earlier, your gains are locked in for you— you are protected against losses—when the market goes down.

The TFRA is a life insurance policy with an expected death benefit and other benefits, such as accelerated benefits for terminal or chronic illness. Like any life insurance policy or annuity, it is not a do-it-yourself investment. I can structure your TFRA with you— setting up the policy correctly in the beginning is very important.

The Earlier the Better

The TFRA is meant as a long-term savings tool. As such, it allows you to save regularly from your already-taxed income into an account that grows over time.

In an ideal world, you would start this investment in your thirties or early forties, many years before you retire. Most people will start it between fifteen and twenty years before their retirement. The key is to give your TFRA plenty of time to compound and earn more money. You might put a thousand dollars per month into it for forty years, and your money is compounding for you all that time. Or you might decide to "max it out" (similar to a 401(k), except the limits can be as high as you want) if you've started later in life.

Whenever you start saving into this TFRA, we always structure it so the death benefit is as low as can be (so the IRS recognizes it as an insurance policy) but still high enough for you to put as much money as you want into it (so you can use it to accumulate a lot of value to fund a tax-free retirement income later on). We don't want it to perform like a bloated mutual fund with tons of fees or a variable annuity that typically has higher fees. We want it to perform like a low-cost index fund.

You might say to me, "John, I get compounding and tax-deferred status in my 401(k). I don't need to do this." The difference in this account is that you're leveraging the rules and laws of life insurance to create an account that virtually has no limits. You're not doing it for the life insurance benefit per se. Life insurance is a nice component of it and, obviously, some people do it for that. But the main benefit and reason why you would have a TFRA is to build up tax-*free*—not just tax-*deferred*—income for your retirement. It also protects you 100% from market risk. The 401(k) is great, especially when there is a match! But the TFRA's tax-*free* component is a very important part of your retirement plan if you want to enjoy a zero or very low tax bracket later on.

Talking about growth in a TFRA, it is usually earning interest every year (except during bear markets, then it just remains flat). After twenty years of funding it, the interest that it's earning would be so high at that point; it's not only easily covering the cost of the insurance, but it's perhaps also earning enough to allow large tax-free loans against the death benefit each year without ever paying them back.

Another big difference with your 401(k) account is in taking a loan against the value of the account. First, when you take a loan from your 401(k) account, you are borrowing against yourself. Secondly, your 401(k) account value goes down dollar for dollar by the borrowed amount, and thus cannot earn interest on any of the borrowed funds.

Secondary Investing Options in a TFRA

Like your 401(k), you can borrow against your TFRA. There are some notable differences, however. Unlike your 401(k), you'll be borrowing from your TFRA without affecting the returns on the face value of the account.

How is that so? If you borrow $100,000 from your $400,000 401(k) account, you leave only $300,000 to profit and grow. If you borrow the same amount from your $400,000 TFRA, you leave the full $400,000 to profit and grow—while you benefit from having the $100,000 to spend or invest elsewhere as you like. This is because with a TFRA, you are borrowing from the insurance carrier and don't touch your own money. You are not borrowing *from* your TFRA; you are borrowing *against* it.

In what scenario, you might ask, would you save hard into a TFRA and then decide to borrow against it? One of the biggest reasons would be because you found another investment that will make you a great return!

Here's a real-life example of how this strategy was used:

During an annual review for a client last year—let's call him Gerald—we found that the TFRA Gerald opened a few years back had now accumulated a sizable $310,000 in the account. At this time he found a completely separate investment that would make him a 15 percent return. He decided to take a $300,000 loan out on his policy, intending to pay it back in 1 year.

Remember that Gerald's original TFRA value is still sitting at $310,000, and the entire amount is still working for him in the external index. With the proceeds of his loan he has now reinvested the $300,000 that he borrowed into a promissory note (or perhaps it was a hard money loan—at any rate, it looked good to him and he went for it). It did in fact give him the 15 percent ROI he hoped for.

When Gerald borrowed the $300,000, there was an interest rate attached to it. The loan from his TFRA was at 3 percent (you pay interest as on any loan, but these are at a lower rate than your bank would offer typically). So, his net return was 12 percent. Not bad!

In parallel, during that twelve-month period, his TFRA earned 14.5 percent interest (which was almost twice what it would ordinarily earn; it would not earn this much every year). You see in the graphic below that he made 14.5 percent, which came to more than $38,000 credited to his account. And so during the review, we saw he had $348,000 in the account at the end of that twelve-month period. What the circle on the left does not show is the money that Gerald had

Policy Values by Strategy
My Investment Summary

$348,700.18

$348,700.18
Total Value

03/21/2022
Next Interest Crediting Date

Start Date   End Date
03/09/2021   03/09/2022

Historical Interest Earned

14.5%	$38,033.02
Index Strategies Weighted Average Credit	Interest Earned

previously borrowed (and still had not paid back into the policy)—$300,000 of the $348,700.18!

Now Gerald had three options: He could pay the $300,000 back on a schedule like a normal loan, he could pay it back on his own schedule, or he could decide not to pay it back at all. What banker gives you those options?

I have a neighbor down the street who borrows from her TFRA every year and puts it in trustee loans that make 10 percent every year for her. This more than covers the cost of the TFRA loan (around 4 percent). She does it every year because she's making money in her TFRA, *and* she's making a net profit in her other investments at the same time.

You might say your money is working twice for you; it's definitely working more profitably.

The only caveat I would give about loans like this is that you really should pay back your TFRA. While it doesn't affect your account value and earnings now, if you don't pay it back, the amount of income you actually get at retirement later is reduced. That said, you pay it back whenever you want. You ultimately control the account.

This approach and benefit are possible due to the IRS rules affecting these accounts. Taking money out of your TFRA is not considered a "loan" from the TFRA or income, according to the IRS. You are not withdrawing the amount in your account. Instead, you are borrowing from the insurance company that issued the policy with a generally favorable interest rate, as my client and neighbor did. This means your policy value never goes down, and the whole amount continues to earn interest and prosper while you use the amount you borrowed for whatever you wish.

In fact, the account balance continues to grow because there won't be an actual "withdrawal" taken until you die. It is only upon your death that the insurance company will subtract the amount you lived off or borrowed from the stated death benefit. Any remaining amount is the final death benefit paid to heirs. Knowing this, what people elect to do instead of leaving a huge lump-sum death benefit to their family of perhaps $3 or $4 million, is use it instead to provide themselves tax-free income in retirement through loans as needed.

Be Your Own Banker

This is how the rich get richer. What this client did with his TFRA loan of $300,000 was make a *secondary* investment from the same cash; his primary investment was still in the TFRA itself. It allowed him to make money in two different places at once with the same capital. What traditional investment account allows you to do that?

Both people I mentioned are taking a loan to make secondary investments with their TFRA, which they determined to be very profitable. Their entire amount of TFRA money was earning all it could, while the secondary investment was also earning all it could for them.

It's a very unconventional way to grow wealth. And it is by no means new. It's also what many people call the infinite banking concept (IBC).

This is also a popular way to fund your business needs—what better secondary investment than your own business? Walt Disney had an account like this, as did J.C. Penney. Mr. Disney used his to help fund his start-up theme park—and we know the continuing success his parks have had around the world. Mr. Penney used his ability to take a loan on his TFRA to resolve momentary company payroll problems at a time of business expansion.

In the case of using the TFRA for business, the fact that you are sinking capital of your own into the business might demonstrate to bankers and other private and institutional funders to do the same. Your TFRA investment could be used as a magnet to obtain other capital.

Wealthy individuals who made political careers have also known about this. John F. Kennedy (of the wealthy Kennedy family) had a TFRA; John McCain had one and borrowed from his to help fund his presidential campaign. Jim Harbaugh, a highly paid college football coach, is also benefiting from this strategy because the University of Michigan is paying millions into a TFRA that he can borrow against tax-free.

So, the ultra-rich use these tax-free retirement accounts very aggressively and successfully. People who want to get wealthy will use the TFRA. Business owners who want to self-fund their business launch or expansion will use them.

The problem with these accounts? The mainstream salaried employee doesn't know they exist! That is simply because, traditionally, the middle-class salaried employee is always taught to put their money in their pensions, 401(k)s, IRAs, and regular stock market or real estate investments. Because of the wealth-growing limitations of those kinds of investments, they stay stuck in the middle class.

We can't do this kind of borrowing for a secondary investment or other expense with a 401(k). We can certainly borrow against the 401(k)—don't get me wrong. As I said, you are reducing dollar for dollar the amount of money working for you in the market.

Another advantage and big difference with borrowing from a TFRA instead of taking out a 401(k) loan is that anytime you get a loan from your TFRA, you're not taxed on it. It is not seen as income by the IRS. Because of that, you're borrowing from your insurance carrier against your policy value (which serves a function similar to collateral).

You can get creative with your loans from the TFRA account. While I recommend to clients that they borrow only to make lucrative secondary investments, it is your money. You can use it as you see fit. As an example, it may be that any consumer loan you are considering comes only with a much higher interest rate than your TFRA loan does; it might therefore make sense to borrow from your TFRA for the following reasons:

- buying new equipment for your business
- funding college tuition for the kids
- making a new car purchase (personal or business)
- paying off a residual mortgage
- making a down payment for the purchase of a new home
- paying sudden out-of-pocket health care costs (either as you are raising your family or later in life for your own health needs)

TFRA and Taxes

The following graphic shows a traditional planning tax picture. Your $79,056 (total income from the first three listed sources) becomes $61,664 (after paying income tax) in a traditional planning process.

SSI Annual	$23,064
Pension	$47,507
Asset Income	$8,485
Federal Tax Rate	$22%
After Tax Income - Current	**$61,664**

By contrast, those who have added a TFRA to the portfolio have removed market risks as discussed, the account grows tax-free, and they are able to take tax-free loans every year. If this retirement plan had a TFRA inside of it, instead of asset income, the tax bracket would likely have been lower as well.

This next example is the income from a traditional portfolio after a 40 percent drop in the stock market (which we have experienced and will doubtless experience again!). Unfortunately, your income drops much more than the market does—over 50 percent more!

After Tax Income - Status Quo	$72,314

After 40% Market Drop

After Tax Income - Downturn	$22,226	-69.26%

As I have said, your TFRA investment is not in the market and not subject to its downside volatility. Every year the index rises, your TFRA experiences growth. And for every year the market goes down, your TFRA will simply go flat or experience no loss due to market fluctuation.

Let's look at the different tax-free income alternatives and how they compare to the TFRA:

TFRA Removes <u>Risk</u> & <u>Taxes</u>

So why is the TFRA the best tax-free retirement income strategy?

Municipal Bonds
- ✘ Low Returns
- ✓ No Market Risk
- ✓ Tax Free

Roth IRA
- ✘ Stock Market Risk (Downturns)
- ✘ Funding Limits
- ✓ Tax Free

TFRA
- ✓ No Market Risk of Losses
- ✓ Virtually No Limits
- ✓ Tax Free

If you are looking for tax-free (and not just tax *deferred*) income in retirement, you have three options: municipal bonds, Roth IRAs, and the tax-free retirement account (TFRA). Municipal bonds and Roth IRAs still have more risk, so it makes sense to discuss with me how to set up and fund your TFRA.

When you are planning for your retirement, you also need to think about how to solve for taxes or what your "net" would look like. A TFRA can greatly reduce or even eliminate your tax burden at retirement. Even if it was just a part of your portfolio, you will benefit from living on a higher level of income while enjoying the tax bracket of someone with a much smaller taxable retirement income. That is why the rich use the TFRA to protect their income from taxes; its allowing them to enjoy a higher net cash flow.

Solving for Taxes
Comparison

	Tax Now	Tax Deferred	Tax Free
2 out of the 3 Investment Buckets are Tax Burdens	• Brokerage • Stocks • Bonds • Mutual Funds • CDs • Savings	• TSP • 401K/IRA • 403(b)/457 • Annuity	• Municipal Bonds • ROTH IRA • TFRA

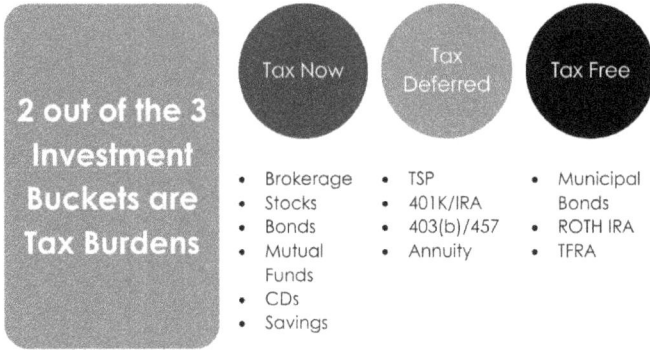

Tax-Free, Flexibility, and Control

Like a Roth, you fuel your TFRA with cash that has already been taxed, then money you take out in loans for retirement income is thus tax-free. Not tax-deferred, then taxable ... but tax-free. This is like double-protection; your money grows with no market risk and when taken out, you get it all.

You also have so much freedom with this option versus traditional 401(k) or IRA accounts. You have *required* minimum distributions (RMDs) from IRAs, 401(k), and deferred pension accounts, meaning by ages seventy-three to seventy-five (depending on what the current law is saying) you are FORCED to take a distribution from your account. Required minimum distribution ages make you start drawing those funds even if you don't need to. But with an IUL life insurance policy, if you want to wait until you're eighty or eighty-five to start borrowing, you can. You're not penalized. It's your account. You can do whatever you want. You don't ever have to take money from it, and if you don't, you will probably leave millions of dollars to your family when you pass away. It's really flexible.

The Benefits of TFRAs

Let me summarize the numerous reasons you should have a TFRA as part of your retirement planning.

These are indexed universal life policies (IULs). Your advisor will choose from A-rated insurance companies that have weathered the highs and lows of markets, any number of wars, and dips and troubles in the economy for well over a century. They are sound. They are reliable over time, which is important if your money is with them for decades!

These are set up to provide maximum tax-free income in the form of loans to you from the policy at whatever age you retire or need the money. It is important to have it set up correctly.

All the money you put into the policy grows when the market rises, maintains its gains during market drops, and when the market rises again, begins where it left off to gain even more.

You have access to the value of your TFRA in the form of loans. These loans are usually at an advantageous rate in relation to the market rate your bank might offer you for the same amount of lending.

Because borrowing from the policy does not reduce your TFRA policy's value, you can make advantageous secondary investments with your loan amount while your policy continues to grow at its original value, not hindered by a traditional withdrawal.

You can pay back these loans on your schedule or not at all. Just know that if you do not pay the loan back when it comes to triggering your tax-free income from it, you will receive a lesser amount than you might have by repaying the loans earlier.

As long as your annual funding of the policy does not exceed the modified endowment contract (MEC) value, you can put as much into it every year as you wish and have access to its tax-free status. Like any investment benefiting from compounding, the earlier you open this TFRA and fund it, the more years it has to grow for you.

The image below shows just one option from one insurance provider. This TFRA is structured to pay in $1000 per month. What happens if you die tomorrow? Remember, this is a life insurance policy. Your beneficiaries receive $846,624 from the death benefit. You'll also notice that this policy has accelerated living benefits, such as chronic or terminal illness benefits, allowing you to accelerate the death benefit if needed. This example also illustrates the tax-free income you might receive at age sixty-seven.

Life Insurance Policy Offers

Die Too Soon

If I Die Tomorrow...
Those I have chosen will receive:

$846,624

Live Too Long

If I Need Cash...
My projected amount of monthly income from policy loans is:
$7,857 at age 67

The projected Cumulative Income for my Policy is:

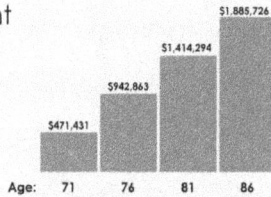

Age:	71	76	81	86
	$471,431	$942,863	$1,414,294	$1,885,726

Become Ill

If I Become Ill...
I can access a portion of my Death Benefit:

The projected Accelerated Benefit Rider Values for my policy at age 67 are:

Terminal Illness Benefit:	$1,158,707 Lump Sum
Chronic Illness Benefit:	$23,476 Per Month
Critical Illness Benefit:	Up to $921,942 Lump Sum
Critical Injury Benefit:	Up to $921,942 Lump Sum

Life Insurance Policy Offers

Premium Allocations	Allocation	Assumed Rate	Current Interest Bonus
Basic Strategy		2.50%	0.35%
Illustrate Systematic Allocation	0%	2.50%	0.35%
Fixed Term Strategy	0%	2.50%	0.35%
S&P 500 Point to Point Cap Focus	0%	5.50%	0.35%
S&P 500 Point to Point Participation Focus	0%	4.50%	0.35%
S&P 500 Point to Point 1% Floor	0%	4.80%	0.35%
Credit Suisse Balanced Trend Index Point to Point No Cap	100%	5.50%	0.70%
US Pacesetter Index Point to Point No Cap	0%	5.77%	0.85%
Total Allocation: 100%			

Typical Annuity Index Options

This is what index returns might look like in a TFRA. The illustration also shows an average return of 5.77 percent. This is quite conservative (low); most years, your TFRA returns can be higher than this, beating inflation and other policy costs. Talk to me about various TFRAs and the returns they provide.

The graphic below shows how the cumulative tax-free income or death benefit at certain ages would look:

Living Benefits of Life Insurance

Current Illustrated Values

Policy Year	Age	Cumulative Premium	Weighted Average Interest Rate	Cumulative Income	Cash Surrender Value	Net Death Benefit
32	71	$672,000	5.36%	$471,431	$985,964	$1,182,992
37	76	$672,000	5.26%	$942,863	$828,155	$929,204
42	81	$672,000	5.19%	$1,414,294	$658,904	$793,011
47	86	$672,000	5.14%	$1,885,726	$473,239	$650,053

The next image shows how the value of your TFRA evolves over twenty-six years of funding with no borrowing and no loans taken. At age sixty-seven, you would start taking loans tax-free.

Policy Year	Age	Premium Outlay	Planned Annual Income	Planned Annual Loan	Accumulated Loan Amount	Accumulated Value	Cash Surrender Value	Net Death Benefit
1	40	$12,000	$0	$0	$0	$6,658	$0	$852,595
2	41	$12,000	$0	$0	$0	$13,296	$0	$859,233
3	42	$12,000	$0	$0	$0	$19,932	$4,629	$865,869
4	43	$12,000	$0	$0	$0	$26,625	$12,228	$872,562
5	44	$12,000	$0	$0	$0	$33,368	$19,918	$879,305
6	45	$18,000	$0	$0	$0	$45,991	$36,601	$891,928
7	46	$18,000	$0	$0	$0	$58,805	$51,141	$904,742
8	47	$18,000	$0	$0	$0	$71,823	$65,960	$917,760
9	48	$18,000	$0	$0	$0	$85,039	$81,046	$930,976
10	49	$18,000	$0	$0	$0	$98,458	$96,419	$944,395
		$150,000	$0	$0				

Policy Year	Age	Premium Outlay	Planned Annual Income	Planned Annual Loan	Accumulated Loan Amount	Accumulated Value	Cash Surrender Value	Net Death Benefit
11	50	$24,000	$0	$0	$0	$117,741	$117,741	$963,678
12	51	$24,000	$0	$0	$0	$137,270	$137,270	$983,207
13	52	$24,000	$0	$0	$0	$157,025	$157,025	$1,002,962
14	53	$24,000	$0	$0	$0	$176,984	$176,984	$1,022,921
15	54	$24,000	$0	$0	$0	$197,125	$197,125	$1,043,062
16	55	$30,000	$0	$0	$0	$223,110	$223,110	$1,069,047
17	56	$30,000	$0	$0	$0	$250,440	$250,440	$831,127
18	57	$30,000	$0	$0	$0	$278,210	$278,210	$831,127
19	58	$30,000	$0	$0	$0	$306,428	$306,428	$831,127
20	59	$30,000	$0	$0	$0	$335,087	$335,087	$831,127
		$420,000	$0	$0				

Policy Year	Age	Premium Outlay	Planned Annual Income	Planned Annual Loan	Accumulated Loan Amount	Accumulated Value	Cash Surrender Value	Net Death Benefit
21	60	$36,000	$0	$0	$0	$369,915	$369,915	$831,127
22	61	$36,000	$0	$0	$0	$405,350	$405,350	$831,127
23	62	$36,000	$0	$0	$0	$441,424	$441,424	$831,127
24	63	$36,000	$0	$0	$0	$478,174	$478,174	$831,127
25	64	$36,000	$0	$0	$0	$515,653	$515,653	$831,127
26	65	$36,000	$0	$0	$0	$553,939	$223,110	$831,127
27	66	$36,000	$0	$0	$0	$593,117	$250,440	$831,127
28	67	$0	$94,286	$94,286	$96,619	$598,845	$278,210	$734,508
29	68	$0	$94,286	$96,619	$197,683	$604,467	$306,428	$633,4447
30	69	$0	$94,286	$101,064	$303,396	$609,959	$335,087	$527,731
		$672,000	$282,858	$291,969				

Typically, I'll illustrate these until age 120.

Overfunding and the MEC

In closing this chapter, I must say two things about building your retirement nest egg through a TFRA.

First, it is NOT a do-it-yourself investment like buying an individual stock. You need to consult with an experienced insurance professional for setting up these accounts.

In planning with my clients, I show them customized growth charts, illustrations, and graphs to illustrate the advantages they will enjoy with the right TFRA. I have robust calculation software to produce the various income solutions possible for your individual circumstances. I am licensed to show you all of the products out there, not just products of one company.

Second, it is not a do-it-yourself program because it is the advisor you choose who keeps you apprised of the IRS limits to funding your TFRA. The IRS (the Tax Code Section 7702 rule I mentioned at the start of the chapter) states that you can overfund such a life insurance policy up to a certain amount. Since this is subject to current federal laws, you need to structure and fund the TFRA correctly; this is why you need a professional to advise you and set it up correctly.

The IRS criteria are summarized in the MEC or Modified Endowment Contract rule. The MEC is the IRS's limit on how much money you can drop into a given insurance policy (in relation to the death benefit) every year without making it into taxable account. Any amount under the MEC maintains the account's tax-free status.

I can't stress enough that it's important to set this up correctly so that you are able to fund it as much as you would like to without going over the MEC limit.

We also structure your TFRA for a *minimum* death benefit and a *maximum* cash value when we create the TFRA for you. This way, you keep the costs down while still putting as much money into it as you can. In other words, the goal is to build cash value; the death benefit also gently rises over a number of years while you build the cash value. Over the accumulation period (fifteen or thirty years—a period decided in advance), you put money into the policy. With all my clients, I build a chart that shows the premium outlay value (how much cash you've put in the account), the accumulation value (how much the account is worth, including earned interest), the surrender value (what you have access to in the form of a loan), the death benefit (since it changes over time as you fund the policy), and annual income (how much tax-free income you can take each year and when that income starts). Each year you own the policy, it earns interest on the account's current value.

What could the retirement income and death benefit look like?

Let's say that you gave your TFRA over thirty years to grow. Upon retirement, you start taking loans as tax-free income from it, say $80,000 per year. That equals $2.4 million that you received in tax-free income over the next thirty years, at which time you die. If the cash value of the account is, for instance, $3.5 million at the time, what happens next? The insurance company would look at the total value of the policy, subtract the total loans as well as accumulated interest on those loans, and then determine the death benefit. In this example, it might be $500,000 after $2.4 million in loans and $600,000 in loan interest are subtracted out. That is what the insurance carrier will pay the beneficiaries.

The primary purpose, then, of investing in a TFRA over many years is, first, to create tax-free income. The additional borrowing capability where you act as your own banker is the second benefit of these accounts.

And of course the tax-free death benefit as well as the chronic and terminal illness benefits are an important part of this account.

5

Choices, Options, Decisions

I OFTEN HEAR PEOPLE PROTEST that they are already contributing to their 401(k) and are "set" for retirement. They don't see how they might need a fixed index annuity to actually produce the income and protect against market downturns. They also might not understand why they should invest for decades in an additional instrument like the TFRA.

I likewise hear people say they have already put their savings into high-yield savings accounts, bonds, or other safe money investments and likewise believe "they are covered for retirement" that way. Then, when we talk about protecting their nest egg as they get closer to retirement, many will say, "Oh, John, no worries. I'm good. I've got lots of time to rebound from this last market loss. I won't be losing my nest egg. No way!"

We also know people who love the stock market and think they are trading whizzes (don't get me wrong—some are!). Then again, there is my client Geoff.

Geoff Protects His Nest Egg

My client Geoff is sixty-seven years old. He had been day-trading in the stock market for many years but had been losing money for a while when he came to me for help. The stock market had seen a major drop, and he was no longer so impressed with his skills and knowledge. It seemed what he knew about making money in the markets only applied to bullish, or rising, market conditions! He had a little over $250,000 in his trading account until the market went down, leaving him only $180,000.

He came to me with three goals: He wanted to grow his funds, have income later on in retirement, and leave a legacy to his two sons. And now? He also wanted complete protection from market downturns!

When he called me, he was motivated to get out of the market. He wanted to transfer his money before he changed his mind because when the market was rising again, he knew he would convince himself to stay in it. But when the market tanked, he would kick himself and ask why he kept doing this! He told me, "I need to get out of stocks. I'm not a professional investor. I need to be spending time with my family. I need to let this money grow and completely protect it."

He decided to set up a fixed index annuity that provided decent growth and had a zero percent floor, so if the market continued to go down, he would not lose a dime. Simply put: When the index went up, on every annual reset, he would get interest credited to his account based on the index performance during that time period. When the market dropped, his account would retain its value, including all prior gains.

He doesn't need the guaranteed income stream immediately; he's just letting his whole nest egg grow. At some future point, if he decides he's going to turn on a guaranteed income stream from the annuity, he absolutely can do that. He could also use it to leave an inheritance for his children, as he wished.

What we set up allowed him to achieve his goals: He didn't want to lose another dime in the market, he wanted his nest egg to grow, he wanted retirement income, and he wanted to leave something to his kids.

Understanding the Upside Potential and Downside Protection of Fixed Index Annuities

People whose only investment experience is in the stock market think there will always be a potential for loss with any other kind of investment. I, therefore, often find myself explaining how there can be no downside, that is, no loss of principal in a fixed index annuity.

But I also find that people don't understand the upside potential very well, either.

The fixed index annuity (FIA) is tied to an external index that mirrors (usually) the S&P 500. It's not directly invested in the market and that is why it doesn't lose money when the market goes down. If the underlying index does well, then holders of a FIA get to participate in a portion of the market earnings.

Let's say the index rises 12 percent. The external index following the S&P 500 might go up 10 percent. Your account will rise 10 percent as well when you are at a 100 percent participation rate. Participation rates vary with each carrier, which is another reason to compare all options.

Now at this point, your account is credited that 10 percent, but then the markets drop dramatically, say 40 percent (which we have seen more than once, by the way). What happens to your account? Nothing. It maintains the balance it had before the drop. In other words, you don't lose a dime when the market takes that 40 percent loss. Everyone in stocks is suffering; you are not.

Let me remind you, there's always a cost to having a guaranteed zero percent floor. And the cost is that you're getting only a portion of the market gains, not all of it. Some annuity options have a zero percent floor, while others have a higher one.

As for the "no downside" aspect of the annuities, the insurance company's typical 1 percent fee charged on your account is used to buy an income rider for guaranteed income, so your true downside is that 1 percent charge if the index were to earn nothing for that period. But it still pales in comparison to the income benefits you'll get from that annuity contract!

Fast forward to when the market starts to rise again. All those people invested in stocks are tense for a long time since their portfolios have to rise to the pre-drop level just to break even. But when the market rises, what happens to your account? It begins to profit again, immediately. You don't need to wait for that breakeven rise. You are already at the pre-drop level, and are able to take advantage of every bit of market increase that occurs. If it takes the market four years (and again, we have seen it before) for the market to reach breakeven for stock investors, you are sitting on four years of new profits!

You are way ahead of everyone holding stocks! When your primary purpose is to protect your money and also make a decent return, you have a lot more peace of mind with these fixed index annuity accounts than just putting everything in the market.

Ensure Your Income Needs Are Met, Then Invest in Riskier Markets

Professional athlete and businessman Shaquille O'Neal invested his money early in his basketball career. His manager told him, "You need to be investing $1 million of your money every single year into *annuities*. Then you can do all of your other investments and whatever you want with the money left over. But do this so you'll be covered after this high-income career is over."

So that's what Shaquille did. He invested that amount into a fixed index annuity every single year. He followed the advice, and now he's got a good number of annuities set up to give him guaranteed income when he decides to trigger them. Even if all his other investments fail, he'll be financially secure the rest of his life. He has guaranteed income he can never outlive. Shaquille actually talks about it when he's interviewed about money and finances.

Managing your own stock market portfolio is one option for retirement. I will never tell you how to invest. However, I'm an avid educator, and I'd like to show you how the fixed index annuities I've talked about compare with the bonds and CDs you might hold.

Bonds versus Fixed Index Annuities

If you are more conservative in your investments and like using instruments such as bonds for protecting your nest egg, I would like to make these precautionary comments. First, between fixed indexed annuities (FIAs) and bonds, which is the stronger candidate for your hard-earned money?

Bonds are described as the asset that investors run toward in terms of financial turmoil. After all, they're backed by the government or big corporations, right? People believe that "when stocks go down, bonds go up," and that may have been true in recent years. But is it always going to be the case?

Since that trend might change, bonds aren't always a smart choice near retirement. As you get close to retirement, your risk tolerance generally goes down. You don't want to risk the large sums of money that you have successfully saved over your working life. When your retirement date is coming up soon (less than five to ten years away), you simply don't have the time to make up for any losses the market may experience. Keep in mind it took about six years for the stock market to recover from its huge 2008 crash.

Nearing retirement, you don't need the scare of such a significant drop in your nest egg!

While government bonds don't have a lot of risks, increasing inflation is also a threat. Inflation will eat away any return that bonds can provide, like any other income you have.

In Favor of Annuities

When investors hold government bonds, they're often left to read the tea leaves to decide what moves central bankers might make. Fixed indexed annuities limit that mystery. If you still need to grow your money to fight the inflation that is inevitable over the coming decades of your retirement, FIAs can be a much smarter choice. Over the past twenty-five years or so, fixed indexed annuities have shown more promise than bonds due to their flexibility.

The significant advantage fixed index annuities offer is that since 2013, most insurance companies have based these products on a *volatility-targeted index*. This is a basket of stocks and bonds designed to reach certain volatility, say 5 percent.

Volatility is calculated by comparing a stock or bond's current output to its historical performance. It is how much statistical "noise" the asset creates over time. By using a basket of products, FIAs can offer their investors no loss of principal while giving some upside associated with stocks.

Volatility targeting means that the company holding the FIA will shift more to bonds in times of market turbulence and more towards stock indices in times of steady growth.

FIA companies have also included the use of "smart beta strategies," or strategies designed to diversify stock portfolios by finding undervalued stocks. Think of it as the *Moneyball* of the stock market.

All these innovations mean that FIA investors can get the best of both worlds—market-based upside profitability and the security of bonds.

As illustrated in earlier chapters, your FIA will provide a return on investment of: (1) more than inflation, (2) growth in value as long as you do not annuitize it, (3) protection from downside market losses, and (4) guaranteed income for life once you annuitize.

Some Annuity Downsides

Let me balance the arguments here! Annuities do have some downsides. With surrender periods and charges, they are *illiquid* assets—wealth you have that can't be turned to cash instantly if you have an emergency without incurring surrender charges. Also, though they are low-risk because the issuer has layers of insurance on itself, they're not *FDIC*-insured. And, of course, there can be fees involved. Variable annuities have very high fees (which, as I've stated in my earlier chapters, I do not recommend to my clients preparing for retirement due to their lesser returns and higher costs).

Annuities have changed significantly since 2013 and offer a sophisticated product that maximizes market upside while protecting investors from downside losses. While they involve fees (I've stated earlier that fixed index annuity fees can be at 1 percent per year while a variable annuity will cost up to 4 percent), you'll have access to a dynamic, risk-controlled portfolio managed by professionals.

Early withdrawal from a fixed annuity attracts penalties, although many types permit you to draw up to 10 percent per year without a penalty. Withdrawing before you are fifty-nine and a half years old can have tax implications if it is from a qualified account.

There is one last option to discuss for investing your retirement nest egg. It comes from people who believe their money is safe and earning enough interest in bank certificates of deposit (CDs) to fund their retirement. Let's see if it is a good option.

Annuity or Certificate of Deposit?

If you want to invest your funds in something other than a 401(k) or IRA, should you choose an annuity or a certificate of deposit (CD)? What are the benefits and drawbacks of each?

Both are insured, and both offer a set return. Annuities are usually insured by the company issuing them and often by state guaranty associations.

Annuities

Annuities offer higher interest rates (in my experience, as high as 6–7 percent in some years) than certificates of deposit, making them better for safe, long-term investment.

Your annuity earns *tax-deferred* interest, meaning that money that would have gone to the IRS as tax can compound, resulting in greater returns. When you start withdrawing, you are taxed at the standard rate. If you funded it with after-tax dollars, you get the principal free of tax.

Annuities are safe from creditor liens in most states. Depending on the options provided by the insurer, you may be able to obtain the following:

- higher payouts if the value of the underlying securities increases while guaranteeing a minimum benefit

- joint-survivor clauses to provide for your spouse after your death

- the option to leave some of the principal to heirs other than your spouse without probate costs

- catastrophe withdrawals, i.e., the ability to draw a large lump sum for emergency expenses

- guaranteed regular payment throughout the annuitization phase

Certificates of Deposit

Banks and credit unions offer CDs. A certificate of deposit is a savings product that earns interest on a lump sum for a fixed period of time. The money must remain untouched for the entirety of the term or risk penalty fees or lost interest. People like them when their bank does not offer high interest savings accounts.

When you take out a CD, you sign an agreement to leave your money in this account for the entire term of the CD in exchange for a set interest rate, protected from fluctuations of the Federal Reserve's rate. Once the time is up, you can withdraw the lump sum from the account, reinvest it in a different CD, or roll it forward for another similar period.

According to www.bankrate.com, in February 2023, the average CD rate (calculated on the one-year rates of ten banks) was 4.12 percent on a one-year certificate.

If you take out a CD from a bank, the FDIC insures it, whereas the National Credit Union Association (NCUA) covers credit unions. Either way, your funds are protected by the federal government up to $250,000. If you need to draw early from a CD, you will pay the penalty, but a lower one than an annuity. Any interest earned is subject to annual income tax.

Certificates of deposit, contrary to annuities, are generally exposed to creditor liens and judgment. In the event of your passing before its maturity date, your named beneficiaries will only receive what is left after any debts on the estate have been paid and will experience a delay and probate costs.

When choosing between an annuity or certificates of deposit as investment instruments, you should primarily consider the purpose of your investment. Annuities are best for supplemental long-term investment goals, such as a retirement that will not run out of funds. Certificates of deposit are best for low-risk investment for medium-term goals, such as a down payment on a house.

6

Some Final Annuity FAQs

THE TYPES OF INSTRUMENTS I'VE PRESENTED here are complex, which is why they are not do-it-yourself, as I've said. Because they are largely unknown to mainstream investors, I'll share here some of the often-asked questions about them.

What If I'm in Poor Health?

If you're in poor health or expect to have a shorter lifespan due to health conditions, this purchase may not be right for you.

These contracts assume that the annuity purchaser is in good health. If you want guaranteed income, you can purchase a five-, ten-, or twenty-year *fixed term* policy. If you and your spouse want to purchase a *joint annuity*, you might want to consider a *life annuity* on the healthier spouse and a *fixed term annuity* for the one in poor health. Additionally, there are special products for people in poor health called *substandard health annuities*. These contracts pay out more money per period than typical policies.

Can I Use 401(K) Distributions to Buy an Annuity?

Purchasing an annuity with a 401(k) distribution allows you to *invest your distribution tax-free* in an instrument that can provide you with a guaranteed income. While this sounds great, there are a few complications.

For example, since the passage of the SECURE Act in 2019, employers now have much more flexibility in including annuity options as part of their 401(k) plans. While combining annuities and 401(k) investments can be a great retirement strategy, the options in your employer's plan might not reflect the full range of annuities on the market.

While most 401(k) plans offer annuity options, they don't do such a great job helping you make the right choice. You recall from earlier chapters that there are hundreds of annuities on the market. It simply is not a do-it-yourself investment or choice. You need to consult a professional (frankly, your plan administrator might not be trained specifically in these products).

Tax Implications of Transferring an Annuity

Transferring an annuity means switching an annuity from one company to another. You can do this as long as it's still in the accumulation phase.

There are a few ways the IRS allows you to do this tax-free. However, most companies have a surrender period, generally about five to ten years. During this period, you must pay a *surrender charge* in order to withdraw your money. Thus, even if you don't have to pay taxes, switching companies can be costly.

When you move your annuity, you generally restart the clock on the surrender period with the new company. Switching companies should only be done after you have read your contract carefully, preferably with a financial professional.

What Are Annuity Income Riders?

"Income riders" are a great way to expand or enhance the features of your annuity. They are always attached to an annuity and not a stand-alone product. Riders are typically separate calculations within your annuity policy. Your annuity statement will list the following:

- accumulation or investment value
- surrender value (the accumulation value minus any surrender fees)
- rider value

Because the rider value is a separate calculation, you can't access it the way you might be able to with a CD. For instance, you might have an income rider that grows your money at an annually compounded 5 percent. Your income payments are based on the compounded amount after you choose to annuitize. However, you don't have access to the full compounded amount if you want to withdraw early.

Income riders typically come with fees that can eat into your annual growth. An annuity professional can help you decide if income riders are right for your needs and then ensure you get the most benefit for the lowest fees.

Cost of Living Adjustment (COLA) Riders

If you're already receiving Social Security payments, you are likely familiar with COLA increases at the end of most years. The administration calculates the rise in the cost of living and adjusts the Social Security amount paid to you. You have seen that in some of my graphics in this book.

A COLA rider in your annuity works similarly to make sure your payments keep up with inflation. Some COLA riders are tied to the Consumer Price Index (CPI). The CPI is a government measure of inflation that sets the COLA for Social Security. While the CPI is a good general measure, it can sometimes *undercount* health care and prescription drug costs. The problem with that? These costs are often a large part of the budget for many retirees!

Other COLA riders increase payments by a set percentage each year. While this ensures you get more money every year, the payments start off rather low. It takes quite a while for the payments to increase to the level they would have been at had you not had the COLA rider. If you have expensive plans early in your retirement, like a big trip or home improvements, this type of rider might not be right for you.

Annuities after Death

If you have a death benefit provision in your annuity, it will pass to your named beneficiary. They can receive the benefits of the annuity as a lump sum or opt to take it over five years or their lifetime.

No matter how they receive the payout, it will be taxed as regular income to them—thus, the advantage of spreading the tax burden over a number of years. The tax burden on a lump sum payment is generally the greatest since the income will likely push the beneficiary into a higher tax bracket.

Additional to that *payout flexibility*, by naming a beneficiary in your annuity contract, you protect them from having to go through the lengthy *probate process*. If your spouse inherits your annuity, he or she can assume ownership and have the same rights and obligations you had when you owned the contract. Any annuity benefits that pass to a beneficiary who isn't your spouse are considered part of your estate for estate tax purposes.

1

Back to Risk Management

PEOPLE LOOKING TO RETIRE in the next few years may find their financial futures clouded by the rising inflation we have been experiencing as I write this and prepare to publish in 2023.

There's no doubt inflation is trending upward at an alarming rate. Consumer prices in the United States rose by an astonishing 9.1 percent in June 2022 alone—the most significant increase since 1981. This becomes all the more disturbing when you consider inflation has seen its largest increase since 1981 every month in the past five months.

As the prices of most food items, utilities, and housing soar, more older individuals are starting to worry about the affordability of a comfortable lifestyle on their fixed income. You may think, "Oh, I've got my CDs," or say, "No problem, since I've got a plush savings account." You may not realize that as inflation continues to rise over the years, interest rates will fall, meaning your financial strategies like CDs and savings accounts won't necessarily generate enough interest to keep you earning a comfortable "wage" after retirement.

As people begin to understand that one important type of risk to their money is inflation, they ask to meet with me. What solutions are available? Having read this far, you know that an alternative investment such as a fixed annuity or fixed index annuity can help you fight inflation risk.

Annuities Protect from Inflation

Fixed index annuities, the FIAs I have spoken about in preceding chapters, offer a middle ground between investing in stocks and choosing a more stable but less growth-oriented form of investment, such as a bond.

Investing in a fixed index annuity can remove market risk from returns while still providing annuity owners with a steady stream of retirement income.

How? Fixed annuity contracts include a guarantee that the insurance company will pay you a fixed, predetermined amount each month—no matter what's going on with inflation.

Before deciding to protect your retirement income by purchasing a fixed index annuity, it's important to make sure you understand the various features and terms associated with annuities.

8

A Glossary of
Annuity Terms

I'M INCLUDING HERE SOME TERMS I used in the book and, while they are common enough to me, are sometimes unknown to my clients!

AVERAGING

Some annuity contracts stipulate that an "average value" will be used to *calculate index-linked interest* rather than examining the specific value on a given date. This "averaging" may occur at the beginning of the term, the conclusion of the term, or at any point in between.

CAP RATE OR CAP

Some annuity contracts feature an *upper limit* on the amount of index-linked interest an annuity can earn. This limit is referred to as the "cap rate" or "cap."

FLOOR

The "floor" is the inverse of the cap rate and signifies the *minimum index-linked interest your annuity can accrue*. The floor is most commonly set at zero percent, though not every annuity contract specifies a floor on fixed index-linked interest.

INDEXING METHOD

The term "indexing method" refers to the approach used to determine how much the index has changed. The most common indexing methods are *annual reset, high-water mark, low-water mark*, and *point-to-point*.

INTEREST COMPOUNDING

"Compound interest" means that any index-linked interest your annuity earns during a term can *earn itself interest in the future*.

Note, however, that some annuity contracts feature "simple interest" instead, which means interest accrued during the term is added at the end of the term but does not itself accrue interest.

MARGIN/SPREAD/ADMINISTRATIVE FEE

In some cases, the index-linked interest is determined by taking a specific percentage off the top of any observed change. This percentage can be referred to as the "margin," "spread," or "administrative fee," and it can either replace or be added to the participation rate.

For example, the change in the index is computed to be 10 percent. Your annuity contract might stipulate that 2.25 percent of this value could be subtracted as an administrative fee. The company won't subtract this fee if the interest rate is a negative value.

PARTICIPATION RATE

The "participation rate" is what determines the percentage of the increase in the index that will then be used to figure out the index-linked interest. For instance, if the index has changed by 10 percent and your participation rate is set at 70 percent, the index-linked interest rate will be 7 percent. Participation rates often have limits to prevent them from being set any higher or lower than a certain maximum or minimum value.

Insurance companies can change the participation rate for new annuities frequently, sometimes as often as daily. That means the participation rate for your annuity can be different from the participation rate of the same annuity issued at a different date. In most cases, the company will guarantee the initial participation rate over a specific period, anywhere from a year to the entire term.

TERM

The index "term" is the period during which the *index-linked interest,* if any, *is calculated.* Any interest that an annuity accrues is usually credited after the term. Most terms run for six or seven years, but they can range anywhere from one to ten years in length.

Some annuity contracts offer single terms, and some designate separate consecutive terms. Most contracts include a window of about thirty days at the end of each term, during which you can choose to withdraw your money without incurring a financial penalty. In the case of installment premium annuities, a new term may begin each time you pay the premium.

VESTING

"Vesting" is another term for *crediting*, and it usually refers to the index paid on an annuity. Some annuities won't vest any interest if you take all of your money out early or will vest only some of it. The vesting percentage usually increases as the term continues and is always 100 percent when it reaches its conclusion.

Author Bio

JOHN STEVENSON is a prominent wealth protection educator and Certified Financial Fiduciary. John has been able to help many people successfully strategize for retirement.

With retirees living longer but also often retiring earlier, having a retirement income they cannot outlive has been a growing concern for many seniors. John's clients include teachers, business owners, executives, doctors, and entrepreneurs, among many others. Not a single client has ever lost money due to market fluctuations.

John is licensed nationally to present insurance solutions to his clients. He is an expert in structuring tax-free retirement accounts, which help his clients build wealth safely and enjoy an extremely low tax burden or even zero taxes in retirement. His services focus on helping people *build a guaranteed retirement*, rather than just leaving retirement finances to chance.

As an avid educator, John actively teaches classes on Social Security, estate planning, and retirement tax planning in universities and colleges throughout Nevada.

He's also a well-known *Retirement & Income Radio* host with thousands of listeners who tune in each week to learn from him.

John knows the importance of helping seniors and families protect against financial downturns. He advises them on ways to have an income they can't outlive and to minimize taxes. He has recently been published with *Think Advisor, Annuity.com, The Annuity Associates, Retire Village, YFS Magazine,* and other publications which have millions of readers worldwide.

Blessed with a beautiful wife and five children, John is happiest when he's spending time with them. When he's not helping seniors and families, he is with his own family or exploring the Sierra Nevada mountains.

Fun Facts about John

- He's a fan of the great outdoors and enjoys hiking, skiing, snowboarding, and backpacking.
- John's a proud Eagle Scout and a dedicated youth mentor.
- He served a two-year mission in South Dakota for the Church of Jesus Christ of Latter-day Saints.
- In addition to his past experience in acting and musical theater, John's an avid singer and was professionally trained by Seth Riggs, who was Michael Jackson's personal coach for many years.